SAMUEL MILLER

As depicted in the 1849 edition of this work.

THOUGHTS ON PUBLIC PRAYER

THOUGHTS ON PUBLIC PRAYER

Samuel Miller

THE BANNER OF TRUTH TRUST

THE BANNER OF TRUTH TRUST

Head Office
3 Murrayfield Road
Edinburgh, EH12 6EL
UK

North America Office
PO Box 621
Carlisle, PA 17013
USA

banneroftruth.org

First published in 1849 by the
Presbyterian Board of Publications, Philadelphia
First Banner of Truth edition 2022
© The Banner of Truth Trust 2022

ISBN
Print: 978 1 80040 282 9
Epub: 978 1 80040 283 6
Kindle: 978 1 80040 284 3

*

Typeset in 11/14 pt Minion Pro at
The Banner of Truth Trust, Edinburgh.

Printed in the USA by
Versa Press, Inc.,
East Peoria, IL

The text reproduced here is largely that of the 1849 edition with only
minor changes deemed necessary by the publisher.

CONTENTS

Foreword by Dr Jonathan L. Master   vii

Dedication   xiii

1. Introductory Remarks   1
2. History of Public Prayer   23
   - Praying toward the East   53
   - Prayers for the Dead   56
   - Prayers to the Saints, and to the Virgin Mary   61
   - Prayers in an Unknown Tongue   64
   - Responses in Public Prayer   72
   - Posture in Public Prayer   73
3. The Claims of Liturgies   83
4. Frequent Faults of Public Prayer   115
5. Characteristics of a Good Public Prayer   141
6. The Best Means of Attaining Excellence in Conducting Public Prayer   169

FOREWORD

I T is easy to find books on preaching. There are good ones from the past and a seemingly endless supply being published today. This is entirely understandable. Preaching the inerrant word of God to the people of God must always be central in the church and in the work of a gospel minister. The words of the apostle Paul make this clear: 'How are they to hear without someone preaching? And how are they to preach unless they are sent? As it is written, "How beautiful are the feet of those who preach the good news!"' (Rom. 10:14, 15).

But along with this, we should also note how Paul outlines the essential components of public worship. He writes, 'First of all, then, I urge that supplications, prayers, intercessions, and thanksgivings be made for all people' (1 Tim. 2:1). Similarly, when the apostles mandate the ordination of the first deacons, they do so because, 'It is not right that we should give up the preaching of the word' (Acts 6:2). Of what does this ministry of preaching consist? 'But we will devote ourselves to prayer and to the ministry of the word' (Acts 6:4). Prayer takes first place for those devoted to preaching, just as public prayer is the priority on Paul's mind when considering public worship.

So where are the books on public prayer? It is surely not the case that the contemporary church already gives sufficient priority to public prayer. If anything, the place of public prayers is diminishing in our congregations. Nor can it be said that our public prayers are of such a high calibre that no instruction is warranted. We know we are deficient. We need instruction on public prayer, and there are few better teachers than Samuel Miller in this little volume.

One reason for the strength of this book is that Samuel Miller, unlike so many, understood the significance of public prayer in the life of a minister. His treatment of the subject begins with the stated conviction that preaching is the great work of the minster, but when comparing it to prayer he writes this:

> It is not wise, however, to exalt either of these exercises at the expense of the other. Both are required in the New Testament church; and both have a value beyond our power to estimate (p. 4).

He knew of that which he wrote. Miller was a devoted pastor in the early years of the American Republic. While he had an interesting literary life, corresponding with Thomas Jefferson and other early American luminaries, what mattered to him most was his work as a gospel minister. He was well-respected by his fellow pastors and he served during years of hardship. Although ministering in a prominent pulpit in New York, both that city and Philadelphia endured epidemics of yellow fever. His older brother Joseph died of the disease. While Miller served faithfully as a pastor in his day, he also looked forward to the future, advocating consistently for and the establishment of what would become Princeton Theological Seminary. After its founding, Miller delivered an address at the inauguration of Archibald Alexander as its first professor. Several years later Miller himself was appointed as Princeton's second professor.

It was against this backdrop of deep commitment to the church and an abiding interest in seeing ministers trained ably for her service that Miller wrote this book on public prayer. It was to these students and to young pastors that he dedicated the volume.

At first glance, some of the topics Miller covers might seem unimportant or perhaps outdated. Readers might be tempted to overlook his discussion about the History of Public Prayer (chapter 2). After all, how many today consider the significance of the correct posture for prayer or wish to examine whether we should pray facing a certain direction? But to pass over these questions would be to miss something important. Not only are these perennial issues within the history of the church from which we can learn, they in fact arise out of assumptions still prevalent today. We still are prone to extremes when it comes to prayer: superstition on the one hand and excessive nonchalance on the other. The misguided principles that undergird our practice of public prayer are often the same as those that lay beneath ancient errors that plagued the church.

When it comes to the remaining chapters of this book, no advocacy is needed. I do not think there is a church-going Christian who will fail to nod in agreement as Miller outlines 'Frequent Faults of Public Prayer' and 'Characteristics of a Good Public Prayer' (chapters 4 and 5). All ministers have something to learn from these instructive chapters. Every congregation would benefit from their application.

Not content with simply correcting errors and diagnosing problems, Miller devotes the final chapter to personally instructing those seeking to improve. Miller shows the vital connection between public and private devotion; the importance of committing God's word to memory; the role of sound Christian literature; and the need for adequate preparation. This is practical wisdom for those who have been persuaded of the many faults commonly found in public prayer and of the great virtues of public prayer that exalts God and edifies his people.

For the good of your soul, for the sake of your ministry, for the health of your congregation, take up this book and read! We must seek to make progress in our public prayer as in all other aspects of our ministry. Miller puts it best when he writes:

> ... no essential improvement will be likely to be made in this department of public service without serious and devoted attention to the subject; without a governing desire to excel; without much communion with the Father of our spirits, and his Son Jesus Christ; and without unceasing application for help from on high. I hesitate not, once more, to apply to this attainment those emphatic words which our Master in heaven applied to another – 'This kind goeth not out, but by prayer and fasting' (Matt. 17:21), (p. 201).

Let us now devote our attention to the great work of public prayer. As we do this, may the God to whom we address our requests revive our other ministerial labours and see fit to answer our requests from on high.

JONATHAN L. MASTER
April 19, 2022
Greenville, SC, USA

DEDICATION

BRETHREN BELOVED IN THE LORD:

Many of you have been my pupils, whom I have followed ever since you left the seminary with which it is my privilege to be connected, with my best wishes, and fervent prayers; and all of you, I doubt not, are willing kindly to receive from an aged servant of the church, who is soon to 'put off this tabernacle,' any intimations which he may deem adapted to promote your acceptance and usefulness.

Unless I mistake, I have observed, from time to time, facts in regard to public prayer which satisfied me that there was a call for special counsel on the subject. It has even occurred to me to doubt whether the well known doctrine of our beloved church, with regard to liturgies, may not have been so rigidly interpreted, and so unskilfully applied, as to lead to practical misapprehension and mischief in regard to the devotional part of the service of our sanctuaries.

It will not surprise me if some of the suggestions found in the following pages, especially in the last chapter, should be considered by some as unexpected, if not as questionable in their character. All I can say concerning them is, that they have not been hastily or inconsiderately made, nor without a sacred regard to those great principles which our venerated fathers regarded as precious, and which were exemplified and recommended by the apostolic church. If I had known of any work adapted to occupy the ground and fulfil the purpose contemplated in the present volume, I should have forborne to trouble the religious community with its publication. But as I am not aware that any such work exists, I am impelled to attempt the service here respectfully offered, which I humbly commend to the patronage and blessing of him who alone can make it useful.

To the *younger* ministers of our beloved church, and to the candidates for the sacred office *alone*, do I venture to present this volume. With regard to the more advanced in life, and the aged, I should be glad, old as I am, to sit at their feet as a learner; and can only beg their candid examination and indulgent estimate of the following attempt to benefit their younger brethren.

I am, my beloved young friends, your affectionate brother in Christian bonds,

SAMUEL MILLER.
Princeton Theological Seminary,
October 31st, 1848.

CHAPTER 1

INTRODUCTORY REMARKS

THE pulpit work of a gospel minister is his great work. True, there are other departments of his labour, the importance of which can hardly be overrated. Family visitation; the catechetical instruction of children and young people; the appropriate instruction and consolation of the sick and dying; the supervision of schools, whether sabbatical or secular, of every kind; and, in short, everything that can be brought to bear on Christian education, and on the moral or religious interests of the souls committed to his care, or placed within his reach—all, all demand his constant and prayerful attention, and can never be neglected without sin, and without the danger of serious injury to the best interests of the flock committed to his charge. Indeed it may be said, with perfect truth, that no one of these departments of labour can be neglected without injury to the minister himself, as well as to those to whom he ministers. These labours out of the pulpit, if faithfully performed, are admirably adapted to prepare and qualify him to fill the pulpit with more skill and more efficiency. How can a pastor preach intelligently and appropriately to his people, without knowing their state? And how is he to know their real state but by more or less intercourse with them in private? And how can he expect to render this intercourse subservient to the great object of his ministry, if it be not essentially and habitually of a religious character? Every time that the pastor goes forth from his study to visit the families of his flock, it ought to be performed for the double purpose of conferring spiritual benefit on them, and receiving a benefit himself. If, for the attainment of the former purpose, he carry the gospel with affection and tenderness on his lips wherever he goes, his own knowledge of the real condition and wants of his people will be greatly enlarged, and his heart warmed: with increasing love to the Saviour, and love and zeal for the salvation of souls, and the enlargement of that kingdom which is not meat and drink, but righteousness, and peace, and joy in the Holy Ghost. O! that ministers could be persuaded to realize that the best part of their preparation for the pulpit, that which is best adapted to impart the richest instructiveness, and the most touching unction to all its teachings, is, not to seclude themselves perpetually in their studies—not to be for ever trimming the midnight lamp; but to go forth and put themselves often in contact with the cavils and the objections of the enemies of the gospel, as well as with the anxieties, the conflicts, the consolations, the joys, and the triumphs of Christian believers.

Still the pulpit work of the minister of Christ is his great work. This view of the subject ought never to be abandoned or forgotten. And to this the ambassador of Christ ought to address himself with all the prayerful diligence; with all the powers of mind, and body, and heart with which his Master has endowed him; and with all those improvements of them severally, which the providence of God places within his reach. And O, if preachers were as earnestly desirous and as faithfully laborious, day and night, to improve every power, intellectual, moral, and physical for this purpose, as the miser is to save and accumulate money, as the ambitious man is to gather and display worldly honours, what progress might we not expect to mark in the character and results of the labours of gospel ministers!

But what department of pulpit work is the most vitally important? and to which ought our main efforts and prayers to be directed? Poor fallible mortals are ever prone to extremes, and, in balancing between attainments and duties, to make sad mistakes in their estimates. The Romanists, overrating the importance of external rites and ceremonies, and laying undue stress on their Missals and Breviaries, have confidently taught that their liturgical performances were far more important than public preaching; and, of course, that the latter might be much more safely dispensed with than the former. And, accordingly, about the time of the rise of the 'Man of Sin,' public preaching was thrust into a corner, and treated as an inferior concern; and, indeed, as to any suitable character of preaching, as an exercise adapted to bring the minds of men into contact with the Holy Scriptures, it was, during the dark ages, in a great measure laid aside. For those, whose policy it was to lock up the Scriptures from the common people, could not, of course, be expected to do anything but discourage scriptural preaching. With a view to justify this estimate it has been said, by those who take this ground, that in

Prayer we speak directly to God, and implore his blessing; whereas in *Preaching* we listen to the speculations of men exhibiting to us their own opinions of truth and duty. They judge, therefore, that if it be necessary or convenient to discontinue either, it is much the less evil to discontinue preaching. And in this judgment some who call themselves Protestants, but who too much resemble Romanists, seem disposed to concur. They deem and pronounce the service of the 'Reading Desk' of far more value, as a means of grace, than the discourses which proceed from the pulpit.

This is, doubtless, a deeply erroneous judgment. Nothing can be more evident than that, in the New Testament history, public preaching makes a much more prominent and important figure as an instrumentality for converting the world, and edifying the church, than public prayer; for it has pleased God, in all ages, eminently 'by the foolishness of preaching' to save them that believe. Nay, more than this, the very statement of our opponents in this argument may be turned against themselves; for if, in prayer, we always *speak to God*, in the way of his own appointment; in preaching, *God speaks to us* by his commissioned servant, if that servant preaches the preaching which the Master bids him. And which is the more serious and solemn employment, our speaking to God, and imploring his favour, or God speaking to us, and communicating his will, either in the language of instruction, of threatening, or of promise? It is not wise, however, to exalt either of these exercises at the expense of the other. Both are required in the New Testament church; and both have a value beyond our power to estimate.

Yet, while we censure Romanists, and others, for under-valuing preaching, we must not excuse Presbyterians if they sometimes appear to undervalue public prayer; and to be less concerned than they ought to be, to secure its rightful and edifying performance. Nothing is more certain than that there is sometimes an appearance of this. It would be difficult to estimate the amount that has been written, by Presbyterians as well as others, concerning the composition and delivery of sermons. Lectures and volumes almost innumerable, have been lavished on this subject; and, in pursuance of their instruction, nothing is more common than to bestow unwearied labour on the preparation of discourses for the pulpit. But how much less of the nature of counsel seems to have been given to candidates for the holy ministry, to aid them in the acceptable performance of public prayer! And how much less attention seems to be bestowed on the part of those candidates, on this whole subject! Books, indeed, in almost countless number, containing forms of prayer, have been given to the public; but books adapted to afford real aid to those who are in a course of preparation for the sacred office, in conducting extemporaneous public prayer in an acceptable and edify-ing manner, have been few and inadequate. Whether this has arisen from an impression that public prayer was a matter of comparatively small importance; or from a notion that it may be safely left, from its nature to take care of itself; or from a morbid desire to recede as far as possible from giving any countenance to prescribed forms, it is not necessary at present to decide. Whatever may have been the reason, it is doubtless, an erroneous one. For whatever comparative estimate we may form, in our wisdom or our folly, concerning two acknowledged ordinances of God, I hope, in the following pages to satisfy every impartial reader, that public prayer is not only a divinely prescribed, but an unspeakably important ordinance; and that both the nature and the means of excellence in the dispensation of this ordinance, are such as not only to admit, but to demand appropriate study, and careful moral and mental culture.

We are, no doubt, warranted in imploring and expecting the aid of the Holy Spirit in every department of our spiritual services. Hence, he who has 'the residue of the Spirit,' speaks of pouring out upon his people 'the spirit of grace and supplication' (Zech. 12:10). And again, it is said, 'the Spirit helpeth our infirmities; for we know not what to pray for as we ought; but the Spirit itself maketh intercession for us with groanings which cannot be uttered' (Rom. 8:27). Yet neither in prayer, nor in any other exercise of religion are we to suppose that the Holy Spirit's influence is intended to supersede the exercise of our own faculties; but rather to stimulate, to strengthen and to purify them. Of course, our petitions for that influence, and our confidence in its aid, so far from forbidding or discouraging efforts to cultivate our minds, and to enrich them with appropriate furniture for leading the devotions of our fellow worshippers, ought rather to excite to unwearied diligence in making the best preparation in our power for discharging in the best manner, this as well as every other duty of the sanctuary. We ought to desire, to ask, and to expect the aid of the Holy Spirit in preaching, and in the prosecution of all our studies and duties. But would any man in his senses imagine that the expectation of such aid was adapted to discourage the use of appropriate means for enlarging and invigorating the mind, and filling it with useful knowledge, and with the materials for the best judgment and taste in divine things? In all spiritual influence, God deals with us as rational creatures; not by superseding or suspending the use of our natural faculties; but by so quickening, elevating, enriching and strengthening them, as to make them capable of greatly improved exercise. I hope, therefore, that every candidate for the holy ministry will bear in mind that as his pulpit work is his great work, so every part of that work is vitally important, and ought to be studied and prepared for, with unceasing diligence. Instead of stopping to balance whether the instruction or devotion of the sacred desk is the more important, or the more worthy of his regard, let him resolve to prepare for both, and to discharge both in the best possible manner. This is the only resolution worthy of him who desires to make the most of every talent he possesses, and of every opportunity he enjoys, for the glory of his Master in heaven.

In regard to the best preparation for leading in social, and especially in public prayer, there are two things worthy of particular notice; the one is what has been called the *spirit*, or *grace* of prayer; the other is what has been denominated the *gift* of prayer.

1. By the *spirit* or *grace* of prayer, is to be understood that truly devout state of mind which corresponds with the nature and design of the exercise. He has the spirit of prayer who engages in that duty with serious, enlightened, cordial sincerity; with that penitence, faith, love, and holy

veneration which become a renewed sinner, in drawing near to God to ask for things agreeable to his will. Even if he have weak intellects, but little knowledge of theological truth, and a very imperfect command of appropriate language, yet if he have a heart filled with love to God, with confidence in the Saviour, and with ardent desires to be conformed to his image, a heart broken and contrite for sin, breathing after holiness, and earnestly desiring the enjoyment of covenant blessings—in a word, a heart in which the Holy Spirit dwells and reigns, that man has the *spirit* of prayer, the *grace* of prayer. Though his words be few, though his utterance be feeble and embarrassed, though his feelings be poured out in sighs and groans, rather than in appropriate language, he may be said to 'pray in the spirit'—to pray in such a manner as will never fail to enter into the ears of 'the Lord of Sabaoth.' Hence we read of the prayer of faith (James 5:15); of the effectual fervent prayer of the righteous man which availeth much (James 5:16); of the spirit of grace and supplication (Zech. 12:10); of the Holy Spirit helping our infirmities in prayer, and making intercession for us with groanings which cannot be uttered (Rom. 8:26); and of God sending forth the Spirit of his Son into our hearts, enabling us to cry, Abba Father (Gal. 4:6).

2. By the *gift* of prayer is to be understood that combination of natural and spiritual qualities which enables anyone to lead in prayer in a ready, acceptable, impressive, and edifying manner; that suitableness and scriptural propriety of matter, and that ardour, fluency, and felicity of expression which enable anyone so to conduct the devotions of

others, as to carry with him the judgment, the hearts, and the feelings of all whose mouth he is to the throne of grace.

These qualities are not always united in those who lead in public prayer. On the one hand, there may be much of the *spirit* of prayer, that is, much of a spiritual and devout frame of mind; much sincerity and even ardour of devotion, where the topics of prayer are not happily selected or arranged; where the language is not well chosen; where the utterance is embarrassed; and where the voice is grating, ill-managed, and unpleasant. So that, while we have no doubt of the sincerity, and even ardent piety of him who leads us to the throne of grace, our pleasure in uniting with him is not a little diminished by the infelicity of his diction and manner. It cannot be doubted, however, that where there is a large measure of the *spirit* of prayer, there we are most apt to find, and commonly do find, a corresponding measure of the *gift* of prayer. On the other hand, there may be much of the *gift* of prayer, where there is, so far as we can judge by appearances, but little of the *spirit*. That is, there may be much skill in the selection of topics, in offering up the prayers of the public assembly; much happiness of expression; much fluency of utterance; and much sweetness and solemnity of voice, where we have reason to believe, there is but little of the spirit of fervent and elevated devotion. I have known a few instances of this kind so remarkable, as to excite universal observation. Nay, I can call to mind one example of the gift of prayer being possessed in a pre-eminent degree, where there was every reason to believe, from subsequent events, that there was no Christian sincerity at all; while I have sometimes seen

men of decided and even eminent piety, who did not appear
to as much advantage in the devotional exercises, as in the
expository and instructive parts of their pulpit work. Even
where liturgy is used, there has often been observed a striking inferiority in the reading of the prayers to the preaching
of the officiating minister. The reverence, the solemnity,
the touching tones which abounded in the latter, were, in
a great measure, wanting in the former. The happy union
of the *spirit* and the *gift* of prayer, is the great object to be
desired, and the attainment of which is so truly important
to the acceptance, and especially to the usefulness of every
minister of the gospel.

There are men in the ministry, as well as out of it—men
no way remarkable either for the vigour of their talents or
the extent of their learning, who, nevertheless, whenever
they engage in social prayer, seem to be eminently in their
element, and we may almost say inspired. So near and
intimate are their approaches to the throne of grace; they
are so obviously and immediately looking into heaven;
so simply filial and tenderly reverential are their appeals
to their heavenly Father; so humble and endearing their
importunity; so full of confidence and joy in a reconciled
God, and of love to an enthroned Saviour; that it is really
adapted to awaken and solemnize the worldly, and to
animate believers to listen to them. O! if our public prayers
were generally and habitually of this character, what impressive and heart-affecting results might be expected!

Now, if this be so, is there not in many who bear the
sacred office, a painful evidence that they have never
paid adequate attention to this important part of the

service of the sanctuary? Are there not found those from whom something better might be expected, who habitually perform this portion of their pulpit work in a common-place, slovenly, and unedifying manner? Is it not supposable, nay, is it not manifest, that public prayer might be made a far more instructive, impressive, and elevating exercise than it is commonly found to be? Who that has been an intelligent and watchful observer of such things, has not known instances in which the *spirit* and the *gift* of prayer, have been so remarkably united and exemplified, as to captivate all hearts, and melt a whole assembly, and to leave an impression more deep and lasting than the most eloquent discourse? If this be so, and if ministers are commonly found to be interesting and useful in proportion to the degree in which they attain excellence in public prayer, then how powerful and solemn are the motives which ought to impel every candidate for the sacred office to aim at a high measure of this excellence, and to employ all the means in his power for attaining it!

The more my attention is directed to this subject, the deeper is my persuasion that a large amount of the defects observable in the performance of public prayer, is to be referred, not altogether or mainly, to the want of piety, nor to the want of rich and varied talents, but to the want of an appropriate and adequate estimate being made of the importance of this part of the public service, and of suitable pains being taken to prepare for its happy discharge. So many examples in proof of this crowd upon my mind, that I cannot help referring to a few of them in confirmation of my statement.

Few divines of the seventeenth century were favoured with higher endowments than the Rev. William Twisse, the first Prolocutor of the Westminster Assembly of Divines. He was fervently pious, profoundly learned, and one of the most acute inquirers and powerful reasoners of his day. In fact, he has been called the Bradwardine of his age. His works, in three volumes folio, form a lasting monument of his vast erudition, and of his uncommonly diversified and vigorous powers of mind. But we could hardly have a stronger proof of the high estimation in which he was held, than the fact that he was selected by the same Parliament which chose and called together the Westminster Assembly of Divines, to preside over the deliberations of that far-famed body, in which he officiated as the presiding officer for about three years.

Such a man might be expected to be gifted and ready in public prayer, as he undoubtedly was in preaching, and in every other part of the duties connected with his profession. But it is plain, from the representation of Baillie, one of the Scottish delegates to the Assembly, that Dr Twisse, with all his accomplishments, was greatly lacking in some of the qualities which are eminently desirable in a good presiding officer, and in none more remarkably than in respect to extempore prayer.[1] In that exercise he would seem, from Baillie's representation, to have been peculiarly deficient. 'The man,' says Baillie, 'as all the world knows, is very learned, very good, beloved of all, and highly esteemed; but merely bookish, and not much, as it seems, acquaint with conceived prayer, and among the unfittest of all the

---

[1] Baillie's Letters, Vol. ii. p. 108.

company for any action. So after the prayer he sits mute.'
To account for this, all that is necessary is to advert to the
fact, that Dr Twisse was bred and ordained in the Church of
England; that he had been accustomed, during the greater
part of the former period of his life, to the use of the liturgy
in public worship; and, of course, had been but little in the
habit of extemporary prayer.[1] And, although it is perfectly
evident, from the proceedings of the venerable body over
which he presided, that his judgment was on the side of
free, instead of prescribed prayer; yet it is probable that,
from want of use, the method of conducting public prayer
extemporaneously was less easy and natural to him than
the use of a form. We have only to suppose this, in order
to account for the fact, that, with all his other pre-eminent
accomplishments, he often appeared to a disadvantage in
conducting the devotions of a public assembly without a
form.

I have heard of a similar defect in the public prayers of
the Rev. President Davies, of our own country, the author of

---

[1] It has been supposed and alleged by many that the members of the
Westminster Assembly of Divines were Presbyterians by prejudice and
by long habit anterior to their deliberations and decisions in that body.
It was, however, by no means so. All the English divines, without a
single exception, who sat in that Assembly, and two of the Scotch, had
been Episcopally ordained; and their early prejudices and habits were
in favour of the prelatical system of government and worship, and not
against them. Some of them, we know, had been long convinced of the
unscriptural character of that system; but others, and not a few, were
brought to the same conviction by thorough and careful examination.
They were evidently led to the views in which they ultimately rested by
mature discussion, and a deliberate examination of God's word.

several volumes of sermons of first rate excellence. It would be difficult to name a collection of published sermons more rich in thought, more sound in evangelical doctrine, and, at the same time, more fervent, animated, and solemn in their whole structure and style. In a word, when I have been called upon by theological students to specify those sermons which I deemed best adapted to popular use, I have felt doubtful whether those of Davies ought not to occupy the very first place in the list. The reader of those sermons would be ready to anticipate for their author not only real but very high excellence in every other part of the public service, as well as in preaching. Yet I have understood, that with all the acknowledged ardour of his piety, and all the rich exuberance of his genius, so apparent in everything that he penned, he was by no means either ready or fluent in public prayer; but was, at least often, hesitating, apparently embarrassed, and far from manifesting that peculiar felicity of thought or expression for which he was so remarkable in his sermons. The probability, indeed, is that President Davies was not a good extemporiser in anything. The tradition is, that he always read his sermons, which, though the universal practice of the established clergy in Virginia, in his day, had been seldom or never allowed among Presbyterian ministers, especially in the middle and southern colonies. Yet still, though he always carried his manuscripts into the pulpit and read his discourses, he read them with a degree of freedom, animation, and fervour which led many good judges to say, that they would almost as soon hear him at any time as George Whitefield. The probability, then, is, that never having cultivated his extemporaneous powers, and having never paid particular attention to preparation for public prayer, his literary sensibility and taste led him often to hesitate in prayer for the selection of appropriate thoughts and expressions, and thus gave rise to the impression, which was undoubtedly made on some minds, that he was less ready, less gifted, and less excellent in public prayer than in preaching. Such a fertile mind and warm heart as his, could not have manifested a want of prompt and appropriate furniture for any part of the public service, if he had been induced early to pay the same degree of attention to it that he evidently had paid to his preaching.

The biography of the late Rev. Robert Hall, of the Baptist denomination in England, records the existence of the same remarkable defect in the public prayers of that eminent man. Few, it is presumed, will hesitate to place Mr Hall very high, if not absolutely at the head, of the eloquent preachers of his day. In some respects, he was considered as superior in genius and in taste to Dr Chalmers; and beyond all doubt, in his resources as an extemporaneous speaker, he had greatly the advantage of his illustrious Scottish contemporary. Yet of this wonderful preacher, his friend and admirer, John Foster, thus speaks in regard to the subject under consideration.[1]

'His manner of public prayer considered as an exercise of thought, was not exactly what would have have been expected from a mind constituted like his. A manner so different in that exercise from its operation in all other employments, could hardly have been unintentional; but on what principle it was preferred, cannot be known or

[1] Hall's Works, Vol. iii. p. 98.

conjectured. But it is to the intellectual consistency and order of his thoughts in public prayer that I am adverting; as to the devotional spirit, there could be but one impression. There was the greatest seriousness and simplicity, the plainest character of genuine piety, humble and prostrate before the Almighty. Both solemnity and good taste forbade indulgence in anything showy, or elaborately ingenious, in such an employment. But, there might have been, without an approach to any such impropriety; and as it always appeared to me, with great advantage, what I will venture to call a more thinking performance of this exercise; a series of ideas more reflectively conceived, and more connected and classed, if I may express it so, in their order.' The writer then goes on to point out, in a diffuse and circuitous manner, what he deems to have been the faults of Mr Hall's public prayers. He supposes their principal faults to have been that they did not abound in connected thought; that they were not adapted to arrest and fix the attention of a worshipping assembly; that they seldom had any sensible connexion with his discourse; and that in intercession, especially for those who might be supposed to be present in the assembly, he was apt to dwell too long, and by excess of personality to encroach on the province of appropriate reserve, and sometimes of strict delicacy. In short, it may be gathered from Foster's statement, that while Mr Hall poured his whole soul, with all its learning, logic, exquisite taste, and fervid feelings into his sermons, he left his prayers to take care of themselves, and bestowed upon them but little thought and no preparation.

I have only to add to this list of illustrious delinquents, the late Dr Chalmers, of Scotland. Perhaps it is not too much to say, that this wonderful man, at the time of his decease, and for twenty years before, had been in some respects, the greatest preacher in the world. In grasp and comprehension of mind; in large, practical statesman-like views on all subjects of ecclesiastical policy; in a capacity for profound investigation; in fervid, overpowering eloquence; and all this united with a simple, childlike piety, it would not be easy to name an equal, or even a second.

And yet, with all this transcendent excellence as a preacher, felt by all, and acknowledged by all who ever heard him, this extraordinary individual, in public prayer was but a common man; nay, scarcely equal to multitudes of inferior men, toward whom but little expectation was directed. One of the most enlightened and ardent admirers of that great man, with whom I have conversed, acknowledged that 'he had not what is commonly called the gift of prayer': insomuch that many strangers who went to hear him, expecting to find him great in everything, and, from his first utterance, deeply interesting, have been ready to doubt whether it was the same man who made the first prayer who afterwards preached, or at least to mark a wonderful disparity between the prayer and the sermon.

It is difficult to account for facts of this sort, without referring them simply to the want of that attention to the subject of public prayer, which is ordinarily necessary to the attainment of excellence in that or in any other department of the public service. True, it may be said, Dr Chalmers seldom allowed himself to utter in public a sentence which he had not written, and was universally known never to excel in extempore speaking. But can it be doubted that the same pre-eminent intellectual vigour, the same ardent piety, and the same peculiar warmth of utterance which gave such a deeply impressive character to all his other pulpit performances, would have been equally effectual in imparting the richest character to all the devotional exercises of the sanctuary over which he was called to preside, if they had been with equal diligence directed to the object?

Nothing can be further from my aim in referring to the cases of these truly great and good men, than to detract in the least degree from their exalted reputation. This would be as unwise, as unjust. My sole object is to impress on the mind of every reader, what I wish to be considered as the leading principle of this volume, viz: that, even in the hands of the most able and pious men, high excellence in public prayer is not, ordinarily, to be attained without much enlightened attention being directed to the acquirement.

There are certain views of public prayer which, however obvious, and however interesting, must be forgotten or overlooked, before slight impressions of its importance, or a materially incorrect estimate of its appropriate characteristics can be admitted. This prayer is, of course, to be considered as the united act of him who leads, and of all who join him in the exercise. Were it to be regarded as merely the vocal utterance of the wants and desires of the individual who presides and leads, it would be by no means invested with the responsible and touching character which really belongs to it. But, when regarded as the joint and humble supplication of hundreds of penitent and believing souls, all engaged in pouring out their hearts to the God of salvation, it assumes an aspect, not only deeply interesting, but eminently adapted to enlist and elevate all the most devout feelings of the worshippers. What an important office does he occupy, who undertakes to be the leader in such an exercise! How full, at once, of responsibility and of interest! what presence of mind, what self-possession, what enlightened and ardent piety, what judgment, what taste, what a delicate perception of the wants and the privileges of the people of God, and what power to express them aright, are indispensable to the appropriate and the suitable discharge of this high duty!

In order to bring to a simple and practical test, what we ought to expect, and what ought to be aimed at in such an exercise, let us imagine that we were listening to an humble, penitent, fervently pious Christian, pouring out his soul to God, in his retired closet, and when he supposed that no other ear than that of his Father in heaven heard his voice. What should we expect to overhear as the utterance of such a heart? Surely we should expect to hear him pouring forth his desires in simple, humble, unaffected terms. We should, of course, expect everything like the glitter of rhetoric, everything like philosophical refinement, or laboured logical distinction, everything approaching the didactic delineation of doctrine, everything, in short, adapted to meet any other ear than that of the God of mercy, or to answer any other purpose than to express repentance toward God, faith in the Lord Jesus Christ, and simple, humble desire for the blessings asked for, to be far away. The moment anything of this kind should be detected in the language, the tones, or the topics of the bending Christian, professing to be engaged in his secret devotion, that moment a chilling doubt would come over us, whether he could be more than half in earnest.

When we apply the same test to a considerable portion of the public prayer in which we are called to unite, can we avoid being driven to the same conclusion? How often, instead of the language of cordial desire, the tones of deep feeling, and the whole manner of importunate suppliants, filled with awe before the majesty of God, and pleading for mercy with all the earnestness of broken and contrite hearts, are we compelled to hear either, on the one hand, effusions in which the invention of the leader is more prominent than his devotion, and sometimes in which the skill of the theologian, and even the taste of the rhetorician are more conspicuous than the mourning for sin, the deep humility and the affectionate confidence of the believer pleading for his life; or, on the other hand, effusions marked by cold and careless indifference, and in which words of course appear to flow from the lips without feeling, and scarcely with conscious purpose!

The model here to be aimed at, and the best means of attaining some degree of conformity to it, will be considered in a subsequent chapter. In the mean time I may be permitted to express deep regret that this subject has not engaged more of the attention of ministers of the gospel, and that there are so many examples of deplorable delinquency in regard to this part of the public service. If it were not so, we should not so frequently find the members of our congregations satisfied if they reach the house of God in time to hear our sermons, after all the preceding prayers are over. If it were not so, we should much more seldom find those who do attend in time to unite in our prayers, gazing about as if they felt no interest in the exercise, or sitting with as much indolence as if they considered what was passing as nothing to them. It will, perhaps, be said that the same gazing about, the same apparent want of interest are often manifested by multitudes, while the best composed liturgy is read. This is, no doubt, true. But the reason of this is, that the formula read lacks that life and power which are adapted to take hold of the minds of men, equally with the extemporaneous prayer. We hold the latter to be inferior to what it might and ought to be, if it be not far more adapted to arrest the attention and impress the mind than any recited form can be.

Nothing can be more certain than that appropriate and adequate attention to this subject would be rewarded with very different results. It may be said, without fear of contradiction, that there is no part of the service of the sanctuary more capable of being moulded to anything that an intelligent and pious heart can desire, or of having stamped upon it a richness and variety; a solemnity, and tenderness; a force of appeal, and a melting pathos which scarcely any other mode of presenting the great principles of intercourse between God and the redeemed soul are capable of having conferred upon them.

The ministers and members of the Presbyterian Church have reason to be thankful that they belong to a body, which is not restrained by any secular power from making such improvements in their system of worship as the word of God, and more ample experience may dictate; and that they are not tied down by ecclesiastical authority to the rigorous use of forms, which some may find a painful burden to conscience. Whatever is most agreeable to the word of God, and most edifying to the body of Christ, we are, happily, at full liberty to introduce, and progressively to modify. Happy will it be for us if we shall be wise enough to make a constant and faithful improvement of this privilege!

If the following pages shall be made by the great Head of the church, in the least degree to promote an increased attention to this part of the service of the sanctuary; to correct, in a single individual, that negligence which has too often obscured the excellence of public prayer; and especially if they shall stimulate any of those who may peruse them, to aim at that elevated character with which the devotions of the sanctuary ought to be, and might be invested, the writer will deem himself richly rewarded for his labour.

CHAPTER 2

HISTORY OF PUBLIC PRAYER

A S prayer is a dictate of nature, as well as a duty required by the express command of our Master in heaven, we may take for granted that it has early and always made a part of the services of public as well as of private religion. Some, indeed, have supposed that social prayer was unknown until the time of Enos, as recorded in Genesis 4:26. But this is by no means probable. As the visible church was constituted in the family of Adam, we must suppose that social prayer in some form was habitually performed. That it entered into the worship of the ceremonial economy of the Old Testament, is abundantly evident, as well from the book of Psalms, as from the historical records of important events during that economy. In the temple service, indeed, there seems to have been no system of common prayer. There were, it is true, 'hours of prayer,' and many and 'long prayers' were there offered up; but these seem to have been by individuals, each one praying for himself, and by himself, and in all manner of words and ways. Of two men who 'went up to the temple to pray,' each one by himself, we have a very graphic account in Luke 17:10. They had in the temple service, sacred music, and sacerdotal benedictions; but never any system of prescribed joint prayer. The ceremonial of the temple was made up of sacrifices, ablutions, burning incense, and minutely enjoined rites of various kinds; but there is not a shadow of evidence that it included a prescribed liturgy, or a system of prepared and commanded devotional exercises. There were, indeed, solemn prayers on special and extraordinary occasions in which multitudes joined; such as those uttered by Solomon (1 Kings 8:22); by king Asa (2 Chron. 14:11); by Hezekiah (Isa. 37:15); by Ezra (Ezra 9:5, 6); and by Jehoshaphat (2 Chron. 20:5). But neither in the daily or the sabbatical service of the temple, as commonly conducted, does there appear to have been any regular or established provision for public or joint prayer; and with respect to the prayers offered on the special occasions above referred to, no one can read them without perceiving that they were extemporaneous effusions, growing out of the occasions which led to their utterance, and which precluded the possibility of their being governed by a previously adapted form.

Public prayer also formed an important part of the service of the Jewish synagogue, that moral institution, which, from an early period, certainly from the time of Ezra, constituted the regular sabbatical worship of the Jewish people. In what manner the prayers of the synagogue were conducted before the coming of Christ, has been the subject of no small controversy. The learned Bingham, in his 'Antiquities of the Christian Church,' and Dr Prideaux, in his 'Connections,'[1] assure us that it was by a regular liturgy.

[1] *Connections*, Part i. Book vi.

The latter professes, with great confidence, to give us, at large, 'eighteen prayers,' which he alleges were in constant use in the synagogue service, long before the incarnation of the Saviour. But if this were so, or if the synagogue worship were conducted by the use of these prayers, or by any prescribed liturgy, it is wonderful that no hint of this alleged fact should be found in the Old Testament history, or in Josephus, or Philo. And, indeed, in the estimation of good judges, these prayers were evidently composed 'at a period when the service of God was no longer kept up in the temple; when the daily sacrifice had ceased; when Jerusalem was no longer their quiet abode; and when the Jews were scattered out of their own land, to the four quarters of the earth. They, consequently, prove the prayers to be posterior to the destruction of Jerusalem.'[1]

The synagogue service was, in substance, the model of the early Christian church. The titles and functions of the officers, and the form of worship were the same. The Jews, indeed, before the advent of the Saviour, had become deeply superstitious, and sunk in heartless formality. They 'loved to pray standing at the corners of the streets,' and 'for a pretence made long prayers'; but the worship of the synagogue seems to have been retained, when our Lord came in the flesh, not, indeed, in absolute purity, but in something of its original character. Accordingly, the Master himself and his inspired apostles were in the habit of attending on its services, and sometimes of taking a leading part in them. In all the accounts which are given in the New Testament history of the synagogue worship, and of the participation

[1] Whitaker's *Origin of Arianism*, p. 301, 302.

in them of the Saviour and his apostles, we do not find the remotest hint of a liturgy, or a prescribed form of prayer. Nor, from any other source have we the least evidence to that amount.

In all the examples of prayer recorded in the Old Testament Scripture, whether public and social, or strictly private and personal, we find nothing like a prescribed form, but in every case the topics presented and the language employed were evidently dictated by the occasion, and flowed spontaneously from the present feelings of the heart. When Solomon, at the dedication of the Temple, in the midst of the congregated thousands of Israel, and on an occasion of transcendent national interest, prayed for the blessing of God on the newly erected edifice, and all who should worship in it, everything that the sacred historian represents him as uttering, seems to have come warm from the heart, and the expression to have been all dictated by the desires and feelings of the moment (1 Kings 8). In like manner, when King Jehoshaphat feared the invasion of a destroying army, he *stood* in the midst of the congregation of Judah and Jerusalem, in the house of the Lord, before the new court, and implored the protection of Jehovah, in a manner which, no reader can doubt, was not the recitation of a form, but the unstudied utterance of the heart (2 Chron. 20). And so, likewise, when Ezra, in a day of rebuke and of spiritual adversity, gathered around him the multitudes of God's professing people, and lifted up his hands, and poured out his soul, as the mouth of the people, both the matter and manner of his prayer plainly evince that everything about it was poured forth extemporaneously, as an expression of the desires and feelings prompted by the solemn circumstances in which he and the people were placed, without being governed by any form or monitor (Ezra 9). The same remarks may be made respecting the prayer of the Levites, who, in the days of Nehemiah, after reading in the book of the law of the Lord their God, confessed their sins, and worshipped the Lord their God. All is apparently unstudied, and prompted by the desires and feelings of the moment. Their prayer was long, minute, entering into a variety of particulars of their history; but throughout bearing the stamp of spontaneous and feeling earnestness (Neh. 9).

The aspect of prayer, under the New Testament dispensation, is marked with greatly increased light, elevation, and enlargement. We find the glorious truths and hopes of the gospel exhibited no longer 'through a glass darkly,' but with 'open face.' Instead of teaching by types, and shadows, and carnal ordinances, everything, under this economy, appears more simple, more spiritual, and more divested of external formality. Surely nothing less and nothing different from this could have been expected under a dispensation in which life and immortality were brought into full light, and in which the infancy of the church had given place to perfect manhood in Christ Jesus. Under this dispensation, of course, we find prayer assuming a language and a tone of more light, enlargement, liberty, and filial confidence.

Who can forbear to marvel then, when the light, the freedom, and the spirituality of prayer have received such manifest and rich improvement under the New Testament dispensation, that there should be any, who, in regard to forms of *praise*, should insist that we are bound still to adhere to the Psalmody of the old economy? What would be thought of anyone who, in preaching and in prayer, should contend that we are not warranted to advance beyond the restricted limits of the ceremonial economy? Why is it not equally wonderful that any, claiming to be eminently evangelical, should occupy this ground with regard to *praise*?

But, while prayer under the New Testament dispensation has received large accessions of light, spirituality, and the spirit of adoption, it is quite as remarkably divested of all restraint and formality. We see a still more marked absence of all confinement to servile forms.

Much use, indeed, in relation to this subject, has been made of the form of prayer which Christ taught his disciples, commonly called the Lord's Prayer. But every circumstance connected with the delivery of that prayer, will convince all enlightened and impartial minds, that it furnishes no proof whatever of either the *necessity* or the *duty* of prescribing set forms of devotion. That it was never designed by our Lord to be adopted as a permanent and precise form of prayer, but only as a general directory, intended to set forth the proper topics, or appropriate matter for prayer, will appear evident from the following considerations.

1. It was delivered by him on two different occasions and for two different purposes. The first time it made a part of the 'Sermon on the Mount,' and was introduced thus—'When ye pray, use not vain repetition, as the heathen do, for they think that they shall be heard for their much speaking. Be not ye, therefore, like unto them; for your

Father knoweth what things ye have need of before ye ask him. After this manner, therefore, pray ye, Our Father, etc.' Here he merely intended to teach them how their petitions ought to be so simply and briefly expressed as to avoid 'vain repetitions.' The next occasion on which this prayer was delivered, was when one of his disciples said to him, 'Lord, teach us to pray' (Luke 11:1). They suggested that this favour had been done by John to his disciples, and desired him to do the same for them. The Saviour then gave, a second time, the substance of what he had given in the Sermon on the Mount, intimating that, in its topics and its simplicity, it was adapted to their then situation. Nothing like rigorous confinement to a verbal form is intimated on either occasion; but the most unlimited freedom and enlargement of diction. For,

2. Though delivered by the Saviour on two occasions, it is not given in the same words by any two of the evangelists. Of course it was not intended to be prescribed as a rigid form.

3. As this prayer was given before the New Testament church was set up, so it is strictly adapted to the old, rather than the new economy. The kingdom of Christ which had long been an object of intense desire to the pious, had not yet been set up. And, therefore, the first petition in this prayer is—*Thy kingdom come!* It is, therefore, strictly speaking, not a prayer entirely appropriate to the New Testament church.

4. There is in this prayer an entire want of what was afterwards prescribed by express precept from the same divine Master, viz.: asking for all blessings in the name of Christ.

Long after he delivered this prayer he said to his disciples, 'Hitherto ye have asked nothing in my name.' He had not yet ascended into the holiest of all, as our Intercessor. But a short time before he ascended to appear in the presence of God for us, he assured his disciples that whatever they asked in his name should be given them (John 16:23, 24). And we are afterwards expressly commanded, 'Whatsoever ye do, in word or deed, do all in the name of the Lord Jesus, giving thanks to God and the Father by him.' Can we suppose then, that a formula intended to serve as a model of prayer in all ages as a strictly verbal form, could be left entirely destitute of this essential feature of Christian devotion? This was not a defect at the time it was given. That great event had not occurred, which would have rendered such a clause then appropriate and suitable. But had our blessed Master intended to prescribe a prayer which it should be incumbent upon his people in all future ages to use, as a complete form, he, surely, would not have omitted this essential reference to his own mediation and intercession.

5. In this form of prayer we have no clause which recognizes thanksgiving for mercies received, which is represented in Scripture both by precept and example, as so important a part of Christian devotion.

Considering this prayer then as a part of the gracious words which proceeded from the lips of the Saviour, it is worthy of our highest regard, and of our diligent and devout study; but to adopt it now as containing all that is necessary to constitute a complete prayer under the full light and claims and privileges of the New Testament economy, must surely be considered as a virtual desertion of principles, which, as Christians, under the present dispensation we must ever acknowledge and hold fast, viz.: that the kingdom of heaven, or the gospel dispensation, is already come; and that no Christian prayer is complete which does not include a reference to the merits and intercession of the great High Priest of our profession. Accordingly,

6. After the resurrection and ascension of Christ, when the New Testament church was formally set up, we read nothing more in the inspired history concerning the use of this form by the disciples of Christ. We have some of their prayers, after those events, recorded. But this is not found among them, and is nowhere referred to in the most distant manner as having been used. Through the many years which the New Testament history embraces, and the many specimens of prayer which it exhibits, we find no allusion, not even the most remote, to the prayer in question. So far as the inspired history informs us, it was never used during the apostolic age, when the religion of Christ appeared among men in its simplest and purest form. We find no evidence of its having been statedly introduced into public worship until several centuries after the death of the apostles; nay, not until grievous superstition and many innovations on the primitive model had crept into the church of God.

From all these considerations, we may confidently infer that the Lord's Prayer was never intended by its all wise Giver to be used as a strict and permanent form; and, of course, that it affords no argument in favour of prescribed liturgies. In this opinion we are fortified by the judgment of many individuals, ancient and modern. The venerable

Augustine, in the fourth century, expresses the decisive opinion that Christ, in delivering this prayer, gave it rather as a directory or general model, than as a form. He says expressly that he did not intend to teach his disciples what words they should use in prayer, but what things they should pray for; and he understands it to be meant chiefly as a guide for secret or mental prayer where carefully selected words are not necessary.[1] In this opinion Grotius concurs, as appears in his commentary on Matthew 4.

Again, there seems to be no hint of the use of precomposed forms of prayer in any of the instances of social worship recorded in the apostolic history. When Peter and John were persecuted and threatened by the Jewish Council (Acts 4:24), when they returned to their companions, the whole company, we are told, with fervent feelings and grateful hearts, lifted up their voices and poured out their humble acknowledgments in language, every word of which bears the stamp of an unpremeditated outburst of spontaneous feeling. He who, on reading the whole narrative, can imagine that they followed in this prayer the words of a prescribed formulary, may be considered as prepared to believe anything that his prejudices can suggest. Again, can anyone imagine that the apostle Paul used a written form when he knelt down and prayed with the elders of Ephesus, on taking leave of them, to see their faces no more? (Acts 20:36). Did Paul and Silas make use of a book when, at midnight, they prayed and sang praises unto God, in the prison at Philippi? (Acts 16:25). Had Paul a liturgy when, at Tyre (Acts 21:5), he knelt down on the

---

[1] De Magistro, Cap, i.

sea shore and prayed with a large body of disciples, with their wives and children, who had kindly visited him and ministered to his wants, when he touched at that city in the course of a long voyage? If so, where and by whom can we imagine a liturgy adapted to such an occasion to have been prepared? Can we suppose that the body of the pious people, male and female, who had assembled at the house of Mary, the mother of John Mark, to pray for the liberation of the apostle Peter, made use of a *form* in pleading for the deliverance and usefulness of that eminent minister of Christ (Acts 12:12)? Is it possible to believe that the church at Ephesus was furnished with a prescribed liturgy, when Paul, in writing to Timothy, while there, thought it necessary to give him such pointed and specific directions concerning some of the topics proper to be introduced into public prayer? Surely if there had been a prayer-book in use there, the directions given in 1 Timothy 2:1, 2, would have been superfluous. All the proper objects of public prayer would, no doubt, have been already provided for. To imagine that such topics had been forgotten, or designedly omitted in an apostolic liturgy, would indeed be a burlesque upon all formularies claiming such an origin.

The truth is, in the New Testament history of the early church of Christ, public prayer is so little prominent, so little is said about it, that it is wonderful any advocate of liturgies should attempt to derive any argument in favour of his cause from that source. Not a syllable is said which gives the least historical countenance to the existence, or the use of any such formularies as the advocates of this cause contend for. It is plain, that the whole subject was left to the disposal of Christian liberty and pious feeling.

Equally without evidence are we that public forms of prayer were in use during the first five hundred years after the apostles.

The advocates of liturgies generally, indeed, assert, without hesitation, that they were in constant use during the period in question. Yet they have never been able to produce the least solid evidence of such a fact. Still they abate nothing of the confidence of assertion. We are reduced, then, to what is commonly considered by logicians as a hard task, viz.: that of *proving a negative*. Yet even this, in the present instance, is an easy undertaking.

When the learned Bingham, in his *Ecclesiastical Antiquities*, and other writers of similar views, assert, and endeavour to prove that liturgies were in constant use in the ages immediately succeeding that of the apostles, they endeavour to make good their assertion by such testimony as the following: That the early Christians had psalms and hymns which had been reduced to writing, which were well known among them, and which they united in singing: that they had, for the most part, a form of words which was commonly employed in administering baptism, and the sacramental supper: that in blessing and dismissing the people, they usually repeated the apostolical benediction, or some received form of expression of an equivalent kind. These writers have not a single fact or testimony to show in support of their assertion but something of this kind. Now it is plain that all this may be granted without in the least degree helping their argument. We, of the Presbyterian

Church, have all these, and yet we are generally considered, and by some reproached, as having no *liturgy*. Nay, we know of no church on earth, of regular organization, that has not psalms and hymns, and substantially a mode agreed upon, and commonly in use for administering the sacraments, without being absolutely confined to a precise form of words. With regard to the use that has been made of psalms and hymns, in this controversy, as affording any countenance, on the principle of analogy, to liturgies, it is too weak and childish to be regarded as at all applicable. How is it possible for a worshipping assembly to unite in singing a psalm or hymn, unless both the words and the tune are previously known and, virtually if not formally, agreed upon? In this case, it is not possible to proceed a step without something prescribed and known beforehand. But all experience proves that no such prescribed form is needful in prayer. A single heart and mouth may utter that in which thousands, if they can hear the voice speaking, may cordially, and without inconvenience, unite.

But the simple and only proper question here is, Had the Christian church, during the first four or five centuries after Christ, prescribed forms according to which she conducted her ordinary prayers in public worship? If she had, it has certainly remained a secret until this time. No hint to that amount has survived in all the remains of antiquity. But so much has survived which speaks a contrary language, that it will prove an easy task to satisfy every impartial inquirer, that, during the period in question extemporary prayer, or, in other words, prayer conducted according to the taste and ability of each officiating minister, for the time being, without being trammelled by imposed forms, was the only method of public prayer in common use in the Christian church.

If there had been in use in the early Christian assemblies, forms of prayer to which their public devotions were confined, prayers would, of course, have been read, as they are now by all who use liturgies. But any expression indicating such a fact, is not found in any of the first five centuries from the apostolic age. The phrases αναγινωσκειν ευχας, or *preces legere*, or *de scripto recitare*, etc., which were so common several centuries afterwards, never, so far as is recollected, then occur in any one instance. We may, therefore, legitimately infer that the thing indicated by such phrases, was neither practised nor known in those times.

But, more decisive still; in describing the prayers then offered, up, the following account is given by some of the earliest and most respectable writers. Justin Martyr tells us, that the president, or presiding minister, in the public worship of the congregation, prayed with his *utmost ability*, (όση δυναμις).[1] Origen speaks of the performance of public prayer in the same manner: 'We worship,' says he, 'one God, and his only Son, who is his *Word* and *Image*, with supplications and honours, *according to our ability*, offering up to the God of the universe, prayers and praises, through his only begotten Son.'[2] And again: 'The Grecian Christians in Greek; the Romans in Latin, and everyone in his own proper language, prays to God, and praises him *as*

[1] Apol. 2.
[2] Contra Celsum, Lib. viii. p. 386.

he is able.[1] The same writer, after speaking of the different parts of prayer, to which it was proper to attend, mentions, first, doxology or adoration, and says, He that prays must bless God *according to his power or ability* (κατα δυναμιν).[2] And in the same work, in a preceding section (the 10th), he says, 'But when we pray, let us not *battologize* (i.e. use vain repetitions), but *theologize*. But we *battologize*, when we do not strictly observe ourselves, or the words of prayer which we express; when we utter those things which are filthy either to do, speak, or think; which are vile, worthy of reproof, and opposed to the purity of the Lord.' Why this caution, if they were furnished with regular prescribed liturgies?

Tertullian, speaking on the same subject, says, 'We Christians pray for all the emperors, etc., looking up to heaven, with our hands stretched out, because guiltless; with our heads uncovered, because we are not ashamed; lastly, without a monitor, because from the heart' (*denique, sine monitore, quia de pectore*).[3] We learn also from Origen, that ministers in his day were accustomed, in public prayer, to officiate with closed eyes, which was wholly irreconcilable with reading a liturgy. 'Closing,' says he, 'the eyes of the body, but lifting up those of the mind.'[4]

Every pastor or bishop, at this time, was considered as charged with the duty of conducting, *according to his own judgment or taste*, the public devotions of his congregation;

---

[1] Ibid. 40-2.
[2] De Oratione, sect. 22.
[3] Apol. cap. 30.
[4] Contra Celsum, Lib. viii. p. 362.

and hence there was great, nay, endless diversity, as now, among those who use extempore prayer, as to the manner in which this part of the public service was performed. Socrates Scholasticus, the ecclesiastical historian, who lived in the beginning of the fifth century, speaking of public prayer, expresses himself in the following unequivocal and strong language: 'Generally, in any place whatsoever, and among all worshippers, there cannot be two found agreeing to use the same prayers.'[1] Surely this could not have been alleged if there had been public, prescribed forms, habitually, or even frequently in use. In nearly similar language, Sozomen, the contemporary of Socrates, and who wrote the ecclesiastical history of the same period, after asserting and describing the uniformity of the public worship of Christians at that time, remarks, that, notwithstanding, 'it cannot be found that the same prayers, psalms, or even the same readings, are used by all at the same time.'[2] In like manner, Augustine, who was contemporary with these historians, speaking on the same subject, says, 'there is freedom to use different words (*aliis atque aliis verbis*), i.e. sometimes in one form of expression, and sometimes in another—provided the same *things* are mentioned in prayer.'[3] And to show that the prayers usually offered up in his day were extemporary prayers, he speaks of some ministers of the sanctuary, 'who might be found using barbarisms and solecisms in their public prayers'; and cautioned those who witnessed them against being offended at such expressions, as God does

---

[1] Hist. Lib. v. cap. 21.
[2] Hist. Lib. vii. cap. 18.
[3] Epistolæ, 121.

not so much regard the language employed as the state of the heart.[1] Chrysostom tells us that, in his judgment, it required more confidence or boldness than Moses or Elias had, to pray as they were then wont to do before the eucharist.[2] But what good reason can be assigned why such confidence or boldness was necessary, if each conductor of prayer had a prayer-book before him, and had nothing to do but to *read* it?

The general fact, that in the early ages of the Christian church, it was left to every pastor or bishop to conduct the public prayers of his congregation as he pleased, that is, as his judgment, taste, and ability might dictate, appears evident from a great variety and abundance of testimony. The circumstances, indeed, which have been already stated, are sufficient of themselves to establish the fact. But many other witnesses might be summoned to prove the same thing. A single one, the venerable Augustine, will be sufficient. That father, having occasion to remark, that some of his brethren in the ministry had many things in their public prayers, especially in the administration of the Lord's supper, which were contrary to soundness in the faith, assigns this reason for it. 'Many light upon prayers,' says he, 'which are composed, not only by ignorant babblers, but also by heretics; and through the simplicity of their ignorance, having no proper discernment, they make use of those prayers, supposing them to be good.'[3] How could this possibly have happened, if the church at that time had

---

[1] De Catechiz. Rudib. cap. 9.
[2] De Sacerdot. Orat. iii. 46.
[3] De Baptismo, contra Donat. Lib. vi. cap. 25.

been in the use of prescribed liturgies? And the remedy which the learned and pious father suggests for this evil, is quite as decisive in its bearing on the question before us, as the statement of the evil complained of. The remedy which he prescribes is, not to take refuge in a written form, or more closely to adhere to such a form; but for the weaker and more illiterate pastors to avail themselves of the counsel and aid of the more wise and learned among the neighbouring pastors, who were qualified to discern and point out any improprieties, and to suggest the best means of avoiding them.

This whole matter will be better understood by adverting to the fact, that, as early as the age of Augustine, many men had crept into the sacred office, and some had even been made bishops, who were unable even to write their own names, and, of consequence, with ease to read writing. This appears, not only from other testimony, but from the records of several ecclesiastical synods or councils about this time, in which bishops, when called upon to subscribe the canons of those councils, were obliged to get others to write their names for them. The following is a specimen of some of the signatures appearing on the records of those councils. 'I, Helius, Bishop of Hadrianople, have subscribed by Myro, Bishop of Rome, being myself ignorant of letters.' Again: 'I, Caiumus, Bishop of Phoenicia, have subscribed by my colleague, Dionysius, because I am ignorant of letters.' These examples of illiterate ecclesiastics, as early as the time of Augustine, serve, at once, to illustrate and confirm the complaint of that father. No wonder that such pastors were unable to conduct the public devotions of their respective congregations in a decent and edifying manner, and, therefore, resorted to such prayers as they happened to meet with, to aid them in their official work. And, no wonder that, in their simplicity and ignorance, they were often imposed upon by imperfect and even corrupt compositions.

It was before stated, that we not only find no traces of any books or prescribed forms of common prayer, in the first five hundred years after Christ; but that we do find a number of facts, incidentally mentioned, which are wholly inconsistent with the use of such books or forms. Some of these facts have been already alluded to, such as the general practice of praying with the eyes closed, and with the hands lifted up, and spread abroad towards heaven. Reading prayers, in these circumstances, was, of course, out of the question. Another very significant fact, explicitly stated, was, that, in the third and fourth centuries, it was not considered as lawful, in any case, to commit to writing the prayers, and other parts of the public service used in administering the Lord's supper. It was not thought proper that any other persons than communicants, for the most part, should be allowed to be present at the celebration, or to be made acquainted with what was said and done in dispensing that ordinance. And, in order to accomplish this concealment, committing any part of these services to writing in any form, was solemnly prohibited. Basil, who flourished towards the close of the fourth century, tells us expressly,[1] that 'the words which they used in blessing the elements were not written; and that what they said both

[1] De Spiritu Sancto, p. 273.

before and after this blessing, were not from any writing.' He says the same concerning the prayers, etc., in the administration of baptism. Now, when we recollect that of all the parts of the public service, as there are none more solemn, so there are none which have been more carefully regulated by prescribed forms, than the administration of the sacraments—insomuch, that several Protestant churches, which have never adopted public forms for other parts of their worship, have thought proper to prescribe them for the celebration of their sealing ordinances; we may confidently conclude that, if there were not, at the period referred to, and, from the nature of the case, could not have been, any written forms for these ordinances, there were none for any other part of the public service. The same fact concerning the unlawfulness of committing to writing the sacramental forms, is attested by many other writers within the first four or five hundred years after Christ.[1] Indeed it was, partly at least, on account of the fact, that the prayers, etc., connected with the administration of the sacraments, were not allowed to be committed to writing, or in any other way divulged, that those ordinances were so commonly, in those early ages, popularly called *mysteries*.

With respect to the alleged liturgies of St Mark, St James, etc., which are found so confidently displayed in Popish, and some other prayer-books, it is believed that all enlightened Protestants give them up as forgeries; and, in regard to the liturgies attributed to Chrysostom, Basil, etc., they are equally discredited by all competent judges. Bishop White, an English prelate, who lived in the stirring reigns

[1] Clarkson's *Discourse on Liturgies*, pp. 38, 39.

of James I and Charles I, delivers the following opinion: 'The liturgies,' says he, 'fathered upon St Basil and St Chrysostom, have a known mother (to wit, the late Roman Church); but there is (besides many other just exceptions) so great dissimilitude between the supposed fathers and the children, that they rather argue the dishonest dealings of their mother, than serve as lawful witnesses of that which the adversary intended to prove by them.'[1]

We read of some of the early churches being supplied with copies of the sacred Scriptures; but not a word of their being supplied with prayer-books in any form. When the buildings in which the early Christians worshipped were seized, and an exact scrutiny made of their contents by the pagan persecutors, we read of copies of the Bible being found, vessels for administering the eucharist, and other articles, very minutely described; but not a hint respecting forms or books of prayer. We meet with frequent instances of reading psalms; reading other portions of Scripture; reading narratives of the sufferings of martyrs; reading epistles from other churches, or from distinguished individuals, but not a syllable of reading prayers. When the multitude of Christians had so increased in Constantinople, that it was thought necessary to distribute them into several churches, the Emperor Constantine was desirous that all these churches should be furnished with the requisite number of Bibles; and wrote to Eusebius, of Caesarea, that copies of the Scriptures should be prepared accordingly. But if public prayers had then been performed by a liturgy, why did not the generous and munificent emperor give orders,

---

[1] Tracts Against Fisher, the Jesuit, p. 377.

at the same time, for a number of prayer-books?[1] Now all this is wonderful, if prayer-books, and reading prayers, had been in as common and stated use as many of the friends of liturgies assert, and would persuade us to believe. The very first document in the form of a prayer-book which we find mentioned in the records of ecclesiastical antiquity, is what is called *Libellus Officialis*, mentioned in the twenty-fifth canon of the Council of Toledo, A.D. 633. This, however, seems to have been rather a brief 'Directory for the Worship of God,' than a form, the use of which, in so many words, was prescribed.[2]

Basil, in the fourth century, giving directions about prayer, remarks, 'that there are two parts of this service; first, thanksgiving and praise, with self-abasement; and, secondly, petition.' His advice is to begin with the former, and in doing it, to make choice of the language of Scripture. After giving an example of his meaning, he adds, 'When thou hast praised him out of the Scriptures, as thou art able' (a strange clause, truly, if all had been prepared and prescribed beforehand, and read out of a book!), 'then proceed to petition.'[3]

The result is, that liturgies were unknown in the primitive church; that, as piety began to decline, and ministers, destitute of the appropriate intellectual and moral qualifications began to multiply, some extra aid in conducting public devotions became necessary; that still it was left to each pastor himself to obtain the aid which he needed, as he

---

[1] Eusebius' Life of Constantine, B. iv. chap. 34.
[2] Clarkson on Liturgies, pp. 14, 15, etc.
[3] Clarkson on Liturgies, p. 120.

thought proper; and that prescribed forms of prayer did not obtain general and established prevalence until the church had sunk into a state of ignorance, darkness and corruption, which all Protestants acknowledge to have been deplorable.

The first account we find in Christian antiquity of a prescribed form for administering the Lord's supper, is that found in the sixth century, by Gregory the Great, bishop of Rome, and commonly called the Canon of the Mass, or a prescribed office for administering the Lord's supper. Gregory, in delivering this formula to the venerable ecclesiastic to whom it was first committed, recognizes the love of variety in public devotions as existing, and as proper to be consulted; declares that he did not wish to be considered as imposing one form only on any part of the church, and that his opinion, as well as his practice, had always been in favour of indulging the love of variety.

In accordance with all this, the celebrated Augusti, a learned German, the author of a work on Ecclesiastical Antiquities, generally considered as the most profound and accurate that any age has produced, decides the question in regard to the existence of prescribed liturgies in the early church, in the following positive and pointed manner:— 'That such an assertion (in favour of the early use of such forms) should have found defenders at an earlier period, when historical criticism was so little practised, is not to be wondered at; but that modern Catholic writers should have ventured to repeat it, is certainly remarkable. The best doctors of that church (the Romish) such as Bona, Bellarmine, Baronius, Le Nourry, Natalis Alexander, Tillemont, Du Pin, Muratori, Renaudot, Asseman, and others, have proved the opinion (of the early existence of prescribed liturgies) to be utterly untenable; and yet, such is the force of prejudice, and such the zeal for favourite hypotheses, that they will not yield even to the clearest demonstrations of an impartial criticism.'[1]

The opinion of Lord Chancellor King, an eminent member of the established Church of England, in his celebrated work on the 'Constitution and Order of the Christian Church, during the first three hundred years after Christ,' is no less decisive. It is expressed in the following terms:

'Now these prayers, which made up a great part of the divine service, were not stinted and imposed forms; but the words and expressions of them were left to the prudence, choice, and judgment of every particular bishop or minister. I do not here say, that a bishop or minister used no arbitrary form of prayer; all that I say is, there were none *imposed*. Neither do I say, that, having no imposed form, they unpremeditatedly, immethodically, or confusedly, vented their petitions and requests; for, without doubt, they observed method in their prayers: but this is what I say, that the words or expressions of their prayers were not imposed or prescribed; but everyone that officiated, delivered himself in such terms as best pleased him, and varied his petitions according to the present circumstances and emergencies: or, if it be more intelligible, that the primitive Christians had no stinted liturgies or imposed forms of prayer.'

'Now, this being a negative in matter of fact, the bare assertion of it is a sufficient proof, except its affirmative can

---

[1] Augusti Denkder Christlichen Archaeologie, iv. 206.

be evinced. Suppose it were disputed whether ever St Paul wrote an epistle to the church of Rome; the bare negation thereof would be proof enough that he did not, except it could be clearly evidenced, on the contrary, that he did. So unless it can be proved that the ancients had fixed liturgies and prayer books, we may very rationally conclude, in the negative, that they had none.'

'Now, as to these prescribed forms, there is not the least mention of them in any of the primitive writings, nor the least word or syllable tending thereunto that I can find; which is a most unaccountable silence, if ever such there were; but rather some expressions indicating the contrary.'[1]

In coincidence with these statements, the learned Clarkson, after his profound investigation of the history of liturgical formularies, comes to the following conclusion: 'And now I may, from the premises conclude, that, for five hundred years after Christ (if not more) the ordinary way of worshipping God in public assemblies, was not by prescribed liturgies. This may suffice, and is sufficient for my purpose. They were not the common usage, while the state of the church was anything tolerable, nor till it was sunk deep into degeneracy. They were not entertained, till nothing was admitted into the church, *de novo*, but corruptions, or the issue thereof; no change made in the ancient usages but for the worse; no motions from its primitive posture, but downward into degeneracy; till such orders took place as respected, not what was most agreeable to the rule and primitive practice, or what was best adapted to uphold the life and power of religion, in its solemn exercises, or what

[1] Inquiry, Part ii. pp. 33, 34.

might secure it from that dead, heartless formality into which Christianity was sinking, and which is, at this day, the sediment of Popery; but what might show the power, and continue the occasion for the exercise of authority to the imperious and tyrannical; or what might comport with the ease of the lazy and slothful, or what might favour the weakness and insufficiency, and not detect the lameness and nakedness of those who had the place and name, but not the real accomplishments of pastors and teachers. In a word, not till the state of the church was rather to be pitied than imitated; and what was discernible therein different from preceding times were wrecks and ruins, rather than patterns.'[1]

But all further argument or testimony on this subject may be spared, since some of the most zealous and competent advocates of liturgies have acknowledged that written forms of prayer had no existence in the apostolic church, nor until several centuries after the apostolic age. Mr Palmer, a minister of the Church of England, now living, who is, perhaps, as zealous and as truly learned an advocate of the rites and forms of that church as any late writer that could be named, acknowledges that, for the first four centuries, there were no written liturgies; but that those who officiated in conducting public prayer, prayed either *memoriter* or extemporaneously.[2] When he speaks of prayers uttered memoriter, it is not easy to define with precision the ideas that he attached to this expression. If he means, as he probably does, that those who led in

[1] Discourse on Liturgies, pp. 181. 197.
[2] Origines Liturgicae i. pp. 9-12.

public prayer, during the first four hundred years, were accustomed to repeat much that rested on their memories which they had read in the Scriptures, or which they had heard from the lips of the eminent men whom they were accustomed to venerate as leaders in that service ; may not precisely the same thing be said concerning a large part of what is called extemporaneous prayer now? Perhaps in regard to those who most eminently excel as leaders in free, social, and public prayer, it has always been true, that nine-tenths of all they ever uttered in this exercise, they had either found resting on their memories from the Bible, or recollected as having been heard from the lips of some respected leader in public devotion. Can any thinking man doubt that the 'memoriter' prayers of the first three or four centuries were to be thus explained? It is quite enough for our purpose, however, to confess, as this writer does, that there was not a single devotional office reduced to writing till the fourth century.

As it is evident from the foregoing statements, that the church made no provision for public formularies of devotion for the first five hundred years after Christ, but that all was left to the discretion of individual pastors; so it is equally evident, that, when liturgies were brought into general and established use, there was no uniformity, even among the churches of the same state or kingdom. The church at large neither provided nor prescribed forms of prayer. Nor did any large portion of the visible church catholic make any such provision. Every pastor in his own parish, and, after Prelacy arose, every bishop in his own diocese, adopted what prayers he pleased; and even indulged to any extent he pleased, his taste for variety. This undoubted fact is itself conclusive proof that liturgies were not of apostolic origin. For if anything of this kind had been known, as transmitted from inspired or even primitive men, it would, doubtless, have been received and preserved with peculiar veneration. But nothing of this kind appears. Instead of this, it is evident, that, as the practice of using written forms gradually gained ground, as piety declined, so the circumstances attending their introduction and prevalence were precisely such as might have been expected. They were adopted, not by the church, but by each pastor who felt his need of them, or was inclined to make use of them. And, by and bye, when bishops were no longer the pastors of single congregations, but were set over larger dioceses, each bishop, within the compass of his own charge, took order in reference to this subject, as his talents or his inclination might dictate. This led, of course, to an almost endless variety. Accordingly, it is a remarkable fact, at once illustrating and confirming this statement, that when the Reformation commenced in England, the established Romish Church in that country had no book of common prayer, no single, uniform liturgy for the whole kingdom, as now; there was a different one for the diocese of every bishop. And, accordingly, when, soon after the commencement of King Edward's reign, the principal ecclesiastical dignitaries of the kingdom were directed to digest and prepare one uniform Book of Prayer for the public service of the church of the whole kingdom, the commissioners appointed for this purpose collated and compared five Romish Missals of the several dioceses of Sarum, York, Hereford, Bangor, and Lincoln, and out of these popish forms compiled their Book of Common Prayer. This book, at first, contained a number of things so grossly popish, that when it was read by Calvin and others, on the continent of Europe, to whom copies were sent for the professed purpose of submitting it to their judgment, and obtaining their opinion, their candid criticisms led to another review, and a considerable purgation.

Calvin, in giving his opinion of this liturgy to Archbishop Cranmer, with perfect freedom and candour, told him that he thought it contained a number of '*tolerabiles ineptias*,' i.e. 'tolerable fooleries,' which ought to be expunged. This was accordingly done. That is to say, the prayers for the dead chrism—extreme unction, and other monuments of Papal superstition with which it abounded, were most of them put out in conformity with his advice. Dr Heylin, himself a most prejudiced and bitter anti-Calvinist, declares, not only that these alterations were made, but that they were made in compliance with Calvin's wishes. 'The former liturgy,' says he, 'was discontinued, and the second superinduced upon it, to give satisfaction unto Calvin's cavils, the curiosities of some, and the mistakes of others, his friends and followers.'[1] The statement of Dr Nichols is to the same amount. 'Four years afterwards,' says he, 'the Book of Common Prayer underwent another review, wherein some ceremonies and usages were laid aside, and some new prayers added at the instance of Mr Calvin, of Geneva, and Bucer, a foreign divine, who was invited to be a professor at Cambridge.'[2]

[1] History of the Presbyterians, pp. 12. 267.
[2] Commentary on the Book of Common Prayer—Preface.

But not withstanding this expurgation of the English liturgy, a number of articles were still left, acknowledged on all hands to have been adopted from the missals of the Church of Rome, which exceedingly grieved the more evangelical and pious portions of the English Church, but which Queen Elizabeth, and the ecclesiastics around her person, refused to modify. Some of these articles have ever since remained in that liturgy, to the deep regret of many good men in the Church of England, and to the equal regret of some on this side of the Atlantic.

It is worthy of notice here, as another fact which goes to establish our main position, that the same general principles which apply to the rise and progress of liturgies in the Romish Church, apply also to the Greek Church. The same late adoption of liturgical formularies in both churches; the same endless diversity of forms when they were adopted; the fact, that their different formularies are entirely unlike, precluding the possibility of their being derived from a common source, and especially an apostolical source; that the most ancient liturgies of each have been denounced by some of its own ministers and members as gross forgeries; and that the best authenticated bear internal marks of being mere human compilations, not authoritative formularies, all serve to show that liturgies were of human, and not of divine origin; and that they took their rise in a declining state of piety. Whoever will be at the pains to consult the profound work of Augusti, the most accomplished modern Christian antiquary, will find all this and more made out with a force of evidence which cannot fail to command the assent of every impartial mind.

Let us now inquire when and how some of the usages in public prayer, which superstition has brought into the church, crept into use in the Church of Rome, and after wards into some other churches, without any authority from the word of God.

PRAYING TOWARD THE EAST

This was a superstition early introduced. It was a practice which the early Christians found habitually in use in the rites of Pagan worship; and it was not long before they began to conform to it, as what they deemed an innocent and expressive usage, and adapted to conciliate their Pagan neighbours. And after adopting it, they speedily began to assign reasons for it, which bore the semblance of Christian principle. In the second century we find an amount of evidence of its existence and general prevalence, which precludes all doubt that it had really crept into extensive use. The reasons given for this superstitious practice by its advocates, are adapted to throw much light on its real character and origin. They are the following:

1. They professed to pray toward the East out of respect and reverence to the Messiah, because they supposed that the East was a title given to Christ in the Old Testament. For that passage in Zechariah 6:12, 'Behold the man whose name is the Branch,' they translated, according to the Septuagint, as they supposed, 'Behold the man whose name is the East.' The original Hebrew word here signifies, arising or sprouting out, as a branch does from a root. The term by which the Septuagint renders this word, is Ανατολη, which, in a large sense, signifies all sorts of arising

or springing out; but, generally and strictly speaking, it is applied to the rising and first appearance of the sun; and, by a metonymy, it is appropriated to the East, because the sun rises in the East. Some of the early fathers, therefore, not knowing the original Hebrew, and finding Christ styled in the popular Greek version, Ανατολη, concluded that, according to the usual signification of the word, he was there termed by the prophet the *East*; and that he was so called because he was to arise like the sun, or, as others said, like a star. 'He is so called,' says Justin Martyr, 'because, as the sun that arises in the East, penetrates through the world, with his warming and illuminating rays; so Christ, the "Sun of Righteousness," when he came, should arise with greater warmth and light, and pierce farther than the material sun, even into the depth of men's hearts and minds.' And again, the same writer says, 'Christ is called the East, because he arose like a star.' And Tertullian calls the East, very emphatically, 'a type of Christ.'

2. Another reason assigned for praying toward the East, by the advocates of the practice, was, that the rising of the sun in the East was an emblem of our spiritual arising out of the darkness of sin and corruption. Thus Clemens Alexandrinus says, 'Let your prayers be made toward the East, because the East is the representative of our spiritual nativity. As the light first arose thence, shining out of darkness; so according to that rising of the sun, the day of true knowledge arose on those who lay buried in ignorance. Hence, the ancient (pagan) temples looked toward the East, that so they who stood over against the images therein, might be forced to look toward the East.'

3. Origen advises to pray toward the East, 'to denote our diligence in the service of God, in being more forward to rise and set about it, than the sun is to run his daily course.' For this he produces a text out of the Apocrypha—Wisdom 16:28—where it is said, 'that it might be known, that we must go before the sun in giving God thanks, and at the day spring pray unto him.'

4. Another reason for praying toward the East, was their opinion of the excellency of that quarter of the compass above all others. This reason Origen thus assigns: 'Whereas there are four points of the compass, North, South, West and East, who will not acknowledge that we ought to pray looking toward the East, symbolically representing thereby our souls beholding the rising of the true light? If any man, which way soever the doors of his house are placed, would rather make his prayers toward the windows, saying, that the sight of the sky hath something more peculiar in it to stir up his affections, than his looking against a wall; or, if anyone pray in an open field, will he not naturally rather pray toward the East than toward the West? and if, on these occasions, the East is preferred before the West, why not so in everything besides? In coincidence with this thought, Augustine remarks: 'When we *stand* at our prayers, we turn to the East, whence the heavens, or the light of heaven, arises, not as if God was only there, and had forsaken all other parts of the world; but to put ourselves in mind of turning to a more excellent nature, that is, to the Lord.'

5. The ancients, in their superstition, had an impression that the East was more peculiarly ascribed to God, because he was the fountain of light; but the West was ascribed to

that wicked and depraved spirit, the devil, because he hides the light, and induces darkness upon the minds of men, and makes them fall and perish in their sin. So Lactantius reasons, when speaking on this subject (Lib. ii. cap. 10).

6. The practice of praying toward the East was probably connected with the ceremony of baptism. It was common in the dispensation of that sacrament, to go through the formality of renouncing the devil and all his works, with faces turned toward the West; and then to turn round and make their covenant with Christ with faces directed to the East. This is frequently mentioned as a fact, by a number of writers in the third and fourth centuries.

7. There is one reason more assigned for this practice, which is, that Christ made his appearance on earth in the East, and there ascended to heaven, and will there appear again at the last day. On all these accounts, and several others which might be mentioned, the practice of praying toward the East has been extensively in use from a very early period, and is still very largely in use among the votaries of superstition.[1] And evidently, like a multitude of practices among the Romanists, it may be traced to a Pagan origin.

PRAYERS FOR THE DEAD

We have no information of this unscriptural and super-stitious practice having gained admittance into the church of Christ prior to the commencement of the third century. True, indeed, the spurious works, known under the name of the Apostolical Constitutions, the works of Dionysius the

---

[1] Bingham's Ecclesiastical Antiquities, B. xiii. Chap. viii. 15.

Areopagite, and the Acts of Paul and Thecla—all refer to this practice as existing at the date of their composition. But all these works have been demonstrated to be the forgeries of times long posterior to the age of the apostles; and, so far as I know, are given up by the great body of learned Protestants of all denominations as utterly unworthy of credit.

Tertullian, early in the third century, is the first credible writer who speaks of the practice of praying for the dead as existing in his time. But we find it in none of the works which he wrote before he became a Montanist; and it has been supposed by many that he learned this superstitious notion and practice from that heretic. It is worthy of remark, however, that Tertullian himself speaks of praying for the dead as practised among the heathen, and that he does not appear to give it his plenary sanction, or to represent it as sustained by the Christian precept or example of any who had gone before him; so that the probability is, that, when professing Christians received the practice, they adopted it from the Pagans.

The doctrine of purgatory very naturally gave rise to the practice of praying for the dead. For if the great mass even of those who were destined to eternal happiness, were considered as entering the eternal world in a state of imperfect sanctification, and were supposed to undergo a certain amount of purgatorial fire before they could be admitted into heaven; and if the prayers of their friends on earth could be regarded as exerting a great influence in shortening the period of this purgatorial suffering; then it would seem that frequent and fervent prayers for this purpose were demanded by every consideration both of benevolence and piety. Accordingly, as early as the beginning of the third century, when this doctrine of purgatory had crept into the church, by the influence of a false and paganized philosophy, we find frequent mention made of prayers for the souls of the departed. And how large a part of the miserable superstition, and the system of unhallowed gain established in the Romish Church, by a mercenary priesthood, has been, for many ages, connected with these unscriptural prayers, is well known.

But the reasons for this practice have not been confined to the doctrine of purgatory. Other considerations have given origin and support to the same practice. These considerations have been such as the following.

(1.) Some of the ancients professed to offer eucharistical prayers for the dead; that is, prayers, consisting in the main of thanksgiving to God for their holy lives; for his many mercies to them, while living; and for their happy deliverance out of this evil world. This is mentioned by Chrysostom, in the fourth century, and by some before, as well as by a number after his day, who professed to give God thanks not only for the martyrs, but for all Christians who departed in the faith and hope of the gospel.

(2.) Another reason for praying for the deceased was, that, as they supposed that all died with some remains of frailty and corruption, so they deemed it reasonable to pray that God would deal with them in mercy, and not with strict justice. And, although many of those who judged and acted thus, fully believed that their departed friends were admitted into heaven; still they saw no incongruity in interceding with God on their behalf, that they might be regarded and treated with unmerited favour. Thus it is humiliating to state, that so enlightened and pious a man as the venerable Augustine evidently prayed frequently and fervently for his devotedly pious mother, Monica, notwithstanding all his confidence that she had been accepted of God, and was resting in peace. While he praised God for her good example, he interceded most earnestly that her mistakes and imperfections might be graciously overlooked.[1]

(3.) Prayers for the dead were intended not only as a testimonial of respect and love for departed friends, but also as an expression of belief in the soul's immortality; to show, as a father of the church in the fourth century expresses it, their belief that the departed had not ceased to exist, but were still living with the Lord.[2]

(4.) As it was the general belief of the church that those who died in the faith and hope of the gospel did not reach the perfection of their happiness and glory until the resurrection, so some thought themselves warranted in having a reference to this in their prayers, and, with this view, beseeching God that the consummation of their blessedness might be hastened in his own time.

(5.) Many of the ancients believed, with some modern errorists, that the souls of all the redeemed (except, perhaps, the martyrs) were confined, out of heaven, in some place invisible to mortal eyes, which they called *Hades*, and sometimes *Paradise*; a place of conscious existence and comfort, where they were looking forward to more complete enjoyment and glory at the coming of Christ. In

---

[1] August. Confess. Lib . 9, cap . 13.
[2] Epiphan. Hæreses, 75.

reference to this imperfect state, it was thought reasonable to pray, that, in the fulness of time, the souls confined in this sequestered state might be brought to the completion of their glory and enjoyment.

(6.) Prayer for the dead finds favour in the *natural feelings* of the human heart. Man is, by nature, a religious being; that is, prone, by the very constitution of his moral and intellectual nature, to grope after future and eternal things. He has, indeed, by nature, no taste for real religion; but sadly the reverse. He loathes it. It is too humbling for him. But superstition is connatural to him; and, where real religion does not reign, will have a place, and exert an influence. Now, natural affection dictates that we retain a lively interest in the welfare of those whom we have loved, who have left us, and gone we know not whither; and a mind ignorant or forgetful of the revealed plan of salvation, will be apt, with its blind yearnings, if it think of praying at all, to pour out supplications in behalf of those who have passed into the presence of him who hears prayer.

(7.) But, perhaps, the most potent of all the influences which have prompted and sustained the practice of praying for the dead, is the claim of ghostly power, and the pecuniary gain of a profligate priesthood, which have been long and essentially connected with it. No wonder that proud and ambitious ecclesiastics have been willing to persuade their deluded votaries that they had a peculiar power, in virtue of their office, to deliver souls out of purgatory by their prayers; and that for this official service they ought to be liberally rewarded. What would the Church of Rome, such as she is, be or do without that enormous system of imposition on the credulity and the pockets of her adherents which has been her support and her stigma for more than a thousand years? Her rigorous exactions on surviving friends, however poor, for masses said for the departed, present one of the most revolting pages in her wonderful history; and the amount of these exactions is so enormous, and forms so large a part of the income of a voluptuous priesthood, as to leave no one at a loss why they are perseveringly continued, and unfeelingly claimed.

PRAYERS TO THE SAINTS, AND TO THE VIRGIN MARY

It is not known that prayers to the saints and to the martyrs appeared, in any form, in the Christian church prior to the fourth, and as some think, the fifth century. And when the practice of offering such prayers did creep in, very different representations concerning their nature and import were presented by those who appeared as their advocates. A majority, it is believed, of these advocates denied that they implied the same kind of worship as that given to Christ, and to the Father; nor were they agreed as to the sense in which the saints and the martyrs were to be addressed and regarded as mediators. The idea, with many, was, that these heavenly inhabitants were to be addressed, not as the authors of any benefit or grace, but as intercessors with God for us; nor even as immediate intercessors, but to pray that the merits of Christ might be savingly applied; and that thus every benefit might be considered as flowing through the atonement and righteousness of the divine Redeemer. But, although we find very different, and not always consistent, representations of this subject in the earliest writers who speak of it, we may consider the practice of praying to the saints and to martyrs as pretty generally established from the fifth century and onward. However the philosophy and the theological aspects of it might vary, the thing itself was all but universal.

The Virgin Mary seems to have been regarded very much as other saints, and prayers to her estimated very much as those to others, until the Nestorian controversy in the fifth century gave a new prominence to her character, and put a new edge on the minds of men in contending for her honours. In that controversy it became, as is well known, a question very fiercely contested, whether it was proper to call the virgin mother of the Saviour, *Mother of God*, or not. Nestorius contended that she ought not to be so called, as she was not the mother of our Saviour's divine nature. The Catholic clergy, however, contended with ardent zeal that it was proper to give her this title. From that time, the authority and power of the Virgin Mary were inordinately exalted; and she became, not only in a degree far greater than ever before, the object of religious worship; but language concerning her began to be indulged of the most idolatrous and shocking kind. She began to be called not only the 'Mother of God,' but also the 'Queen of Heaven'; and, indeed, sometimes to be addressed as if she had an authority and power above the Saviour himself. Hence, in praying to the Virgin, it became customary to say to her 'command your Son'—exercise the authority of a mother over her son in requiring your Son to do this or that.' From that time to the present it has been the constant practice in the Romish Church not only to make the Virgin Mother by far the most prominent saint in the whole calendar, but to make her the object of the most unlimited idolatry; to call upon her every hour to guide, enlighten, protect and save; to beseech her to make her Son according to the flesh propitious; and, in fact, to speak of her, and to her, as if she held the reins of universal empire.

It is unnecessary to say to those who have the word of God in their hands, that for nothing of this kind is the least countenance found in Holy Scripture. Nothing is more clearly laid down in the inspired oracles than that God is the only proper object of religious worship; that all prayer addressed to creatures is idolatry; and that this is not only a departure from that which is right, but has been pronounced by a God of infinite holiness to be an aggravated sin in the sight of him who has declared that he will not give his glory to another. Are saints in glory omniscient or omnipresent? Can they hear our prayers? Can they help us if they did hear them? And is not every such prayer a virtual insult to him who has proclaimed himself the only Mediator between God and man; and who has commanded us to ask for everything in the name of Christ, and to rely for audience and acceptance only on his atoning sacrifice and prevalent intercession?

And as to the Virgin Mary, we do not find the least countenance in sacred Scripture for the idolatrous worship of which we have spoken. Neither Jesus himself, nor his inspired apostles ever commanded or even encouraged Christians to give more honour to the Virgin Mary than to any other woman who did the will of God. But we do find in the sacred history facts and statements which are wholly irreconcilable with the Romish practice on this subject. How do we find Jesus himself treating his mother on several occasions recorded by the evangelists? Does he recognize her right to rule over him, or to prescribe his course of action? True, indeed, in his early youth, we are told he dwelt with his parents, and was 'subject unto them.' But in this statement no distinction is made between his mother and his reputed father. He was 'subject to *them.*' But does his manner of addressing his mother, when she found him in the temple, 'sitting among the doctors'; when he spake to her at the marriage in Cana of Galilee; when she, with others, came to him when he was preaching in a crowded assembly; and when he committed her to the care of the 'beloved disciple,' while hanging on the cross, appear to recognize in her that authority over him which Romish idolatry ascribes to her? Far from it. We have but to look into the sacred history, to see that on every occasion of which a record is made, the Saviour treated his mother according to the flesh with pointed respect and filial reverence; but, in no case, as if he thought she had the least right to exercise authority in regard to his official and public conduct.

PRAYERS IN AN UNKNOWN TONGUE

Nothing can be more evident than that, in the apostolic church, and for a number of centuries after the apostolic age, the public prayers were always conducted in the vernacular tongue of the worshippers. In regard to the practice of the apostles, the language and the reasoning used in the 14th chapter of the First Epistle to the Corinthians, throughout, are so perfectly clear and conclusive, as to banish all doubt in reference to their example. The apostle speaks of praying and prophesying in an unknown tongue with such unequivocal and severe censure, as to show that he regarded it with entire disapprobation, not only as an absurdity, but as utterly defeating the great design of social worship. And, with respect to a number of centuries afterwards, nothing is more certain than that the primitive practice was adhered to with uniform strictness. Of this we have so many testimonies, in the form either of direct assertion, or of manifest implication, as to preclude the possibility of mistake in regard to the practice for a number of centuries.

That the church, both before, and for some time after the establishment of Christianity in the Roman empire, should have thought proper, throughout the greater part of western Christendom, to make choice of the Latin language as the vehicle of her devotions, was not surprising. It was the vernacular tongue of a very large portion of her members, and both convenience and pride dictated its use. But that she should still insist on the use of this tongue, in all her public prayers, long after it had ceased to be vernacular to a very large portion of her worshippers; when, perhaps, not one in an hundred, or perhaps five hundred, of those who repeated those prayers, had any proper understanding of the import of the words which they uttered, is a most signal example of adherence to speculative system, at the expense of reason and of all practical utility.

It may not be altogether useless to inquire into the motives which have induced the Church of Rome to adopt this absurd and cruel system of compelling her people to attend on prayers which they do not understand.

(1.) Probably one motive was, that they might cast an air of antiquity over their whole system. This the Papacy has always affected. It has ever been a favourite object with the followers of the 'Man of Sin,' to represent their worst errors and superstitions as coming down to them from the primitive church, and as sanctioned, if not authoritatively appointed, by the apostles. This notion, they supposed, would be, of course, promoted by the constant use of a language which wore an antiquated aspect, and which has long since ceased to be popularly spoken. 'The Latin,' say they, 'is an ancient language, and the Church hates novelty, and desires to have everything savouring of antiquity.'

(2.) Another reason which has been given for the prescribed use of an unknown tongue in public devotions in the Romish Church, is, that that community may have the appearance of being one and the same all over the world; that the worshipping assemblies of that denomination, whether in Italy, in Germany, in France, in England, or the United States of America, might all be found speaking the same language in prayer, using the same forms, and recognizing their relation to the same great body, wherever they might sojourn or reside. They forget that this is not the unity of which the Bible speaks. They forget that, according to the word of God, there may be great diversity of dialect, where there is entire unity of faith, and hope, and love, and obedience; and that where this exists, diversity of articulate speech is no obstacle to all that is mainly valuable in the communion of saints.

(3.) Perhaps the fact that the Latin Vulgate was the only Bible authorized to be in common use among Romanists, was not without its influence in prescribing the language of their public prayers. As that version was made their standard Bible, by a decree of the Council of Trent, we cannot wonder that they aimed at the miserable consistency of having their prescribed forms of devotion in the same language, that the one might be just as intelligible to the common people, or rather as unintelligible, as the other.

(4.) Another plea employed is, that living languages are in a state of constant fluctuation. New words are every day introduced, and old words and phrases changing their meaning. Now, say they, since religion and all its offices ought to be fixed and immutable things, they ought to be embodied in a language as fixed and unchangeable as the system which it exhibits.

(5.) It is not necessary, they tell us, that we should understand what we utter in public, if our hearts be only sincere.

(6.) Finally: there is no want of charity in believing that one leading purpose in pursuing this practice, is to keep the people in ignorance, and to make them constantly more dependent on their priesthood. That 'ignorance is the mother of devotion,' may be considered as a leading Popish maxim; and, truly, of the greater part of the devotion which exists in that communion, we have reason to believe it is the real and legitimate mother. No intelligent judge of their arts and habits can doubt, that one leading object of the whole, is to increase the power of a corrupt and tyrannical priesthood; to impress the mass of the people with a deep sense of their prerogatives and their power; and to extort from them a more blind and implicit homage. The votaries of Antichrist, instead of opening the Scriptures to the people, and trying to bring them in contact with all minds within their reach, rather make it their study to lock them up from the laity, either by entirely prohibiting their perusal, or hiding them from the popular mind by the cover of a dead language. If it were their policy to prevent the common people from reading and understanding the Scriptures, it was natural that the same policy should also dictate a system of management to make them the blind and submissive repeaters of a form of words of which they understood nothing.

As to the real character of this practice, nothing can be plainer than that it is contrary to reason, to Scripture, and to the early judgment and practice of those who now glory in it.

(1.) It is contrary to reason—to common sense. The great object of language is to communicate thought. Of course, if it be not understood, it communicates no thought. What would be deemed of a lawyer, pleading before an earthly court, in which the English language alone was spoken, who should speak Greek, or Latin, or Hebrew, of which not one in a thousand of his hearers understood a word? If he insisted on employing a language thus unintelligible to his hearers, and refused to employ any other, would he not be deemed insane? Surely it is not less unreasonable to insist on retaining in use a plan by which millions of Romanists in every part of the world continue daily, under the guise of worshipping God, to repeat, parrot-like, a form of words which conveys no intelligible ideas either to themselves or others.

(2.) It is contrary to Scripture. The apostle, in the chapter before referred to,[1] declares that he had rather speak five words which were understood, than ten thousand in an unknown tongue. He speaks of himself as being a barbarian to those whom he addressed in a tongue unknown to them; and much more would this be the case if it were unknown to himself as well as to them. And, accordingly, on the day of Pentecost, when multitudes were assembled in Jerusalem, from every part of the Roman empire, that no portion of the people might, be permitted to listen to an unknown tongue, a direct miracle was wrought, and the apostles had the gift of tongues imparted to them, enabling them to speak to everyone that heard them 'in that tongue in which he was born.' Surely this fact is adapted strongly and conclusively to discountenance the Romish practice.

The following remarks by the pious and amiable Dr Doddridge, in his Family Expositor, on the 13th and 16th verses of this chapter, are so judicious and pointed, that I cannot forbear to transfer them to this page.

'Had the most able and zealous Protestant divine endeavoured to expose the absurdity of praying in an unknown tongue, as practised in the Church of Rome, it is difficult to imagine what he could have written more fully to the purpose than the apostle has here done. And when it is considered how perversely the Papists retain the usage of such prayers, it will seem no wonder they should keep the Scriptures in an unknown tongue too. But they proclaim at the same time their superstition and idolatry in so universal a language, that even a barbarian might perceive and learn it

[1] 1 Cor. 14.

in their assemblies. Let us pity and pray for them, that God may give their prejudiced minds a juster and happier turn. And since we see the unreasonable and pernicious humour of immutably adhering to ancient customs, prevailing to maintain in the Church of Rome so flagrant an absurdity as praying in an unknown tongue, let it teach us to guard against every degree of the like disposition; and not so much consider what hath been the practice of any church, in which we were educated, or have chosen to worship, as what the reason of things, and the authority of Scripture concur to dictate.'

(3.) Finally, the present practice of Papists is entirely opposed to the early example and practice of the church in the city of Rome. The bishop of Rome claims to be infallible, and the community over which he presides, claims to be also, infallible; and, if so, of course, ever the same, from the time of the apostles to the present hour. Now it is well known that the church in Rome, during the first few centuries, never thought of using any other language, in any part of the public service, than the vernacular tongue. How, then, is it consistent with her infallibility now to act a different part? On every account, then, it appears that this superstitious practice is worthy of condemnation. It is opposed to reason, to scriptural precept, to scriptural example, and to the invariable usage of the best and purest churches in the ages nearest to the primitive times. And nothing can be clearer than that its continuance is adapted to enslave the mass of the people; to perpetuate ignorance and error; and to render it more easy for a corrupt and tyrannical priesthood to lord it over their deluded followers.

If any attestation to the truth of these statements should be deemed desirable, the following extract from the recent history of the eminently learned Neander, bearing on an allied subject, viz. reading the Scriptures in the vernacular tongue, will be considered as conclusive. It relates to the first three centuries.

'The reading of the Scriptures was of the greater consequence, since it was desired to make every Christian familiar with them; and yet, on account of the rarity and high prices of manuscripts, and the poverty of a great proportion of the Christians, or because all could not read, placing the Bible itself in the hands of all was out of the question. The frequent hearing of the word, therefore, must, in the case of many, be a substitute for their own reading it. The Scriptures were read in a language that all could understand. This, in most of the countries belonging to the Roman empire, was either the Greek or the Latin. Various translations of the Bible into Latin made their appearance at a very early period, since everyone who had but a slight knowledge of the Greek, felt the want of thus making himself familiar with the word of God in his native tongue. In places where the Greek or the Latin language was understood by only a part of the community, the men of education, the rest being acquainted only with the ancient dialect of their country, which was the case in many cities in Egypt and Syria, church interpreters were appointed, as they were in the Jewish synagogues, who immediately translated what was read into the provincial dialect, that it might be universally understood.'[1]

[1] General History of the Christian Religion and Church, by Dr Augustus Neander, Vol. i. 303. Torrey's translation.

RESPONSES IN PUBLIC PRAYER

Nothing of this kind existed in the apostolic church, nor for several centuries after the apostolic age. The entire silence of the best authorities on the subject, plainly shows that nothing of the sort had any place in Christian worship for a number of centuries after Christ. The responsive form of worship seems to have been originally confined to the music of the church, and only transferred at a much later period, and probably by an insensible transition, to the other portions of the public service. This agrees perfectly with the well known circumstance, that some parts of various existing liturgies, which, in modern practice, may be 'either said or sung,' are always 'sung' in the more solemn, and what claims to be the more ancient method of performance, as, for example, in the cathedral service of the Church of England, as compared with the ordinary parochial service. Accordingly, a very large part of the actual service in the public worship of the Romanists may be considered as falling under the description of church music.

The earliest information I can find in respect to responsive worship, seems to have reference to the alternate chants or canticles introduced, at an early period, from the Syrian into the Western Church, and especially associated with the name of Ambrose, and the practice of the church of Milan, and hence popularly called the Ambrosian Mass. It seems probable that responses in prayer originated from this ancient mode of singing; and gradually made their way into popular use. But, assuredly, there is no trace of them in the primitive church. Chanting prayers, and responses in prayer, equally unknown in the apostolic age, had, probably, an allied origin.

POSTURE IN PUBLIC PRAYER

This is not essential. A prayer truly spiritual and acceptable may be offered up in any posture. And yet this is, undoubtedly, a point by no means unworthy of consideration and inquiry. There are certain proprieties of gesture in all public performances in which it is desirable that all who frequent our religious assemblies should be agreed both in principle and practice. The ancient Christians made it a subject of specific regulation; and there is a manifest advantage in having those who worship together uniform in their external habits, as well as in their theological creed.

The postures in prayer, as laid down in Scripture and early usage, are four—prostration, kneeling, bowing the head, and standing erect. The examples of all these are many, and leave no room to doubt that they were all practised, and are all significant and admissible.

(1.) *Prostration.* This seems to have been reserved for days of special humiliation and mourning. Thus Joshua and the elders of Israel, when they had suffered a sore defeat by the men of Ai, continued a whole day, from morning till eventide, prostrate on their faces before the ark, with dust on their heads, in the exercise of the deepest humiliation and prayer (Josh. 7). Joshua also himself, on a preceding occasion, when filled with alarm, 'fell on his face to the earth, and did worship' (Josh. 5:15). Thus also, David and the elders of Israel, when the aspect of God's providence toward them was peculiarly alarming and awful, fell on their faces to the ground, and worshipped (1 Chron. 21:16). The patriarch Job, too, when the bereaving dispensations of a sovereign God, fell in thick succession upon him, acknowledged his power, and prayed to him in a similar posture (Job 1:20). Nay, even our blessed Saviour himself, in his agony in the garden, fell prostrate on the ground, and poured out his soul in the most moving manner to his Father in heaven.

This posture in prayer is, undoubtedly, not suited to ordinary worship. It may answer for a deeply penitent individual, in his private apartment, burdened with an unusual sense of sin, or overborne with an awful sense of the divine glory. Or it may be assumed by a body of penitent worshippers in the open air, when placed in circumstances which call for special humiliation, which seems always to have been the situation of those who are recorded to have used it; but is by no means adapted to the case of an assembly in an edifice such as we ordinarily occupy. In fact, in many cases, in such an edifice, this posture would be physically impossible, and ought not to be attempted. It befits only one, or a small company, in an agony of peculiar contrition, or transported by the enjoyment of special manifestations of the divine favour.

(2.) *Kneeling* is the next of the four postures becoming in prayer. Of this we have many examples in sacred Scripture. They, chiefly, though not exclusively, belong to cases of individual and private devotion, or to small circles engaged in prayer on special occasions. Thus the prophet Daniel 'kneeled down on his knees,' in his private chamber, three times a day, and prayed. The Psalmist exclaims, 'O come, let us bow before the Lord, let us kneel before God our Maker.' Stephen, at his martyrdom, knelt down and prayed. Jesus himself, when he was withdrawn from his disciples 'about a stone's cast, kneeled down and prayed.' The apostle Paul twice knelt down and prayed with circles of praying friends, who had come together to testify their respect to him—once at Miletus, on his way to Macedonia, and once at Tyre, on his journey to Jerusalem (Acts 20:36; 21:5). This is, undoubtedly, a significant and becoming posture in prayer, strongly expressive of humility, reverence and earnestness. It is the usual and becoming posture in secret and family prayer, and by many generally used in small circles engaged in social prayer.

(3.) *Bowing the head.* This may be considered as a kind of intermediate attitude between kneeling and standing. There is frequent reference made to it in Scripture; as, for example, in Genesis 24:26, in which we are told of Abraham's servant, that when he went to Padan Aram on an interesting errand for his master, and when he observed what he considered as manifest tokens of divine guidance and approbation, he 'bowed his head and worshipped the Lord.' This appears to have taken place in the open air, at the well of water, when surrounded by those who were watering the cattle, and when, perhaps, few, if any, of those who were standing by had their attention drawn to this act of obeisance. The same is said of the elders of Israel in Egypt: 'When they heard that the Lord had visited the children of Israel, and that he had looked upon their affliction, they bowed their heads and worshipped.' Again, in the days of King Hezekiah, on an occasion of grateful interest, when the house of God was cleansed, 'the king and the princes commanded the Levites to sing praise unto the Lord, with the words of David and of Asaph the seer; and they sang praises with gladness, and they bowed their heads and worshipped.' This easy and convenient method of manifesting a spirit of devout reverence, may be employed at all times, and in all circumstances, when the worshipper is standing erect, and when neither prostration nor kneeling could be without great difficulty adopted.

(4.) *Standing* is the fourth and last of the attitudes becoming and adopted in public devotion. And this, it is well known, was the posture adopted in the Church of Scotland; by our fathers, the Puritans, in England; and by the descendants of both churches on this side of the Atlantic. There is much to recommend this posture. We spontaneously rise in the presence of a superior. It is expressive of respect and reverence. We have also many examples of this in Scripture. When Solomon, in the midst of the thousands of Israel, made a prayer at the dedication of the temple, while the king himself knelt down on a platform of brass, all the people around him *stood up*, while they united with him in addressing the throne of grace (2 Chron. 6:3, 13). When Jehoshaphat proclaimed a fast, and offered up a solemn prayer, in the critical circumstances in which he and his people were placed, we are told that he *stood upright*, and that the whole multitude, not only the men, but their wives and their children, all *stood* and prayed (2 Chron. 20:5, 13). We know, too, that the usual posture in public prayer, in the Temple, and afterwards in the Synagogue, was that of *standing*. This practice was evidently adopted in the early Christian church. The following testimony from Lord Chancellor King's 'Inquiry into the Constitution of the Primitive Church within the first three hundred years after Christ,' is decisive in regard to this point. 'As soon as the sermon was ended, then all the congregation *rose up* to present their common and public prayers unto Almighty God, as Justin Martyr writes, that when the preacher had finished his discourse, "they all *rose up*, and offered their prayers unto God"; standing being the usual posture of praying (at least the constant one on the Lord's day, on which day they esteemed it a sin to kneel), whence the preacher frequently concluded his sermon with an exhortation to his auditors, to *stand up* and pray to God, as we find it more than once in the conclusion of Origen's sermons; as, for example, "Wherefore, *standing up*, let us beg help from God, that we may be blessed in Jesus Christ, to whom be glory for ever and ever, Amen!" And again, in another place; "Wherefore, *rising up*, let us pray to God, that we may be made worthy of Jesus Christ, to whom be glory and dominion, for ever and ever, Amen!" And again, "Standing up, let us offer sacrifices to the Father through Christ, who is the propitiation for our sins, to whom be glory and dominion, for ever and ever, Amen!"'[1]

Testimony to the same amount, and of the same explicit character, is found in the writings of Jerome, Augustine, Basil, and Epiphanius, from all which sources we learn that the *standing* posture in public prayer was regarded as a real privilege which was denied to those who had incurred the discipline of the church, and who returned to her bosom

[1] Inquiry, chap. ii.

as penitent. They were compelled to *kneel*, as a testimony of deep humiliation; it being the prerogative and the right of believers only, and consistent professors of religion, to occupy the standing posture in their public devotions.

Nay, this matter was deemed of so much importance as to be made the subject of solemn regulation by the first General Council that ever assembled in the Christian world. The Council of Nice, which was called together, A.D. 325, to dispose of the heresy of Arius, after its decision on that important subject was disposed of, passed a number of canons in regard to points which were considered as calling for authoritative direction. In the twentieth of these canons it was ordained, that all kneeling in public prayer be prohibited on the Lord's day, and on any day during the fifty days between Easter and Pentecost, or Whitsuntide. The Lord's day, which commemorated the resurrection of the Saviour from the dead, and which, on that account, they regarded as a season appropriated to spiritual joy and rejoicing, they considered as forbidding a posture of humiliation. And so the fifty days between Easter and Pentecost, the one intended to commemorate the resurrection of Christ from the grave, and the other, the outpouring of the Holy Spirit on the apostles. On these joyful days, all kneeling in public prayer was expressly forbidden, as unbecoming the privileges and the hopes of the Christian. On the other hand, they deemed the erect and joyful posture of standing altogether unsuitable for those who appeared in the sanctuary as penitents, to whom a posture indicating humiliation and shame was more appropriate. *They* seem to have been compelled to kneel at all times.

Thus it is incontrovertibly evident that, for the first three hundred years after Christ, standing in public prayer was the only posture allowed, on the Lord's day, to the mass of Christian worshippers, who were in a state of union with the church.

In all Presbyterian churches standing is regarded as the appropriate posture in prayer at all times. This posture is recommended by a variety of considerations. (1.) It was evidently the apostolical and primitive plan. (2.) The first General Council, as we have seen, in the fourth century, enjoined it by a solemn canon. (3.) It is a posture expressive of respect and reverence. (4.) It is adapted to keep the worshipper wakeful and attentive; while the postures of kneeling and sitting are both favourable to drowsiness.

'It is a mistake,' says Mr Trench, 'growing out of forgetfulness of Jewish and early Christian customs, when some commentators see in the fact that the Pharisee prayed *standing*, an evidence manifesting his pride. Even the parable itself contradicts this notion; for the Publican, whose prayer was an humble one, stood also. But to pray standing was the manner of the Jews. See 1 Kings 8:22; 2 Chron. 6:12; Matt. 6:5; Mark 11:25. True, in moments of more than ordinary humiliation or emotion of heart, they changed this attitude for one of kneeling or prostration; see Dan. 6:10; 2 Chron. 6:13; Acts 9:40; 20:36; 21:5. Hence the term *station* (*statio*), passed into the usage of the Christian church on this account. It was so called, as Ambrose explains it, because, *standing*, the Christian soldier repelled the attacks of his spiritual enemies; and on the Lord's day the faithful *stood* in prayer to commemorate their Saviour's resurrection on that day; through which they who by sin had fallen, were again lifted up and set upon their feet.'[1] It is to be remembered, that this testimony is from the pen of a distinguished clergyman of the Church of England.

The posture of *standing* has been objected to by some on two grounds. First, as fatiguing to the feeble and infirm. But, if the officiating minister be tolerably discreet in the length of his prayers, this objection can have little or no force to those who are in ordinary health. It will, surely, rather be a relief than otherwise to stand up ten, or, at most, twelve minutes, when the sitting posture is to be maintained during almost the entire remainder of the time allotted to the public service. It has also been alleged, in the second place, that the standing posture is unfavourable to close and solemn attention; that it tempts him who maintains it to look about him. But if there be really a devout spirit, and a disposition to depress the countenance, to withdraw the eyes from surrounding objects, it is easy to see that the objection before us may be as perfectly obviated as in any other posture.

The posture of *sitting* in public prayer has no countenance either from Scripture, from reason, or from respectable usage, in any part of the church's history. It was never allowed in the ancient church, and was universally regarded as an irreverent and heathenish mode of engaging in public devotion. True, if there be any worshippers so infirm from age, or so feeble from disease, that standing erect would really incommode or distress them to a degree unfriendly to devotion, let them sit; not in a posture of indifference or

---

[1] Trench on the Parables.

indulgence; but with bowed heads, and fixed countenances, as becomes persons reluctantly constrained to retain such an attitude, and who are yet devoutly engaged in the service.

It were greatly to be wished that this matter should engage the attention of pastors and church sessions to an extent commensurate with the evil to be remedied, and which is evidently gaining ground. Thirty or forty years ago, nineteen out of twenty of all Presbyterian worshippers were in the constant habit of standing in public prayer. Nothing else was thought of; and if anyone was constrained by debility or sickness to remain sitting, he felt as if his posture needed an apology. Such a case was an exception to a general rule. But the practice of indulging in this posture has gradually made so much progress, that sitting has almost become the general rule, and standing the exception. Now, when we cast an eye over many of our worshipping assemblies, we see a large portion of the professed worshippers not only sitting, but sitting in such a posture of lounging indulgence, as evinces that nothing is further from their minds than a spirit of devotion. This surely ought not to be so. It is unscriptural, unseemly, and highly revolting. Where there is really a spirit of devotion, there will be some manifestation of it in the outward posture. And where the outward posture is unfriendly to such a spirit, it will, in spite of any professed wish to the contrary, speedily banish it. Unless ministers, then, are willing that the members of their flocks should gradually fall into habits in the highest degree unfavourable to the spirit of devotion, let them raise their voices against this growing evil. Let them warn their hearers against the indulgence of a spirit of lounging indifference in the house of God. Let them proclaim, that, even when standing erect may cost some effort, and be attended even with some pain, this very circumstance may tend to obviate drowsiness, and to keep the mind more intent on the solemnity and importance of the exercise. It is, undoubtedly, desirable that there be uniformity in our habits of worship. This uniformity is not likely to be attained or established without the employment of means for the purpose. Every pastor is responsible for much in this respect, and has much in his power. Let him drop a hint in the pulpit, and let him impart a suggestion, now and then, to young and old in his parochial visits, and he may generally arrest undesirable practices in the bud, and keep most external habits in a state of decorum and order.

CHAPTER 3

THE CLAIMS OF LITURGY

IN the foregoing history of public prayer, much has been said which bears on the question of *liturgies*; but that whole question is so important in relation to the best method of conducting the devotional exercises of the sanctuary, that a formal discussion of it is evidently demanded in the course of the examination before us.

The word *liturgy* is derived from two Greek words, λειτος, *public*, and εργον, *work*; importing, of course, public work, or the performance of sacred public offices; which may be considered as comprehending, in a large sense, the whole ceremonial of public worship; including, among Romanists, the mass, with all its accompaniments; but, among Protestants, the term is commonly employed to express the forms adopted and prescribed, by any church for conducting her public, devotional and sacramental services. Concerning these there is great diversity of principle and practice among the various Protestant denominations. In some, there are formularies rigidly prescribed, and exclusively adhered to in every part of the public service. This is the system of the Church of England, and of her daughter, the Episcopal Church in the United States. In some other churches, these formularies extend only to the administration of the sacraments, the celebration of marriage, the burial of the dead, and the prescribed forms for sacred praise; leaving all the other devotional exercises of the sanctuary to be conducted extemporaneously, according to the discretion of each officiating minister. This, it is well known, was, substantially, the plan adopted by the French, the Helvetic, the Genevan, the Dutch churches, and many of the churches of the German Protestants. It is also the plan of our Methodist brethren in the United States. While, by a third class, as among the Presbyterians of Scotland and the United States, the Independents of England and America, and some other Reformed churches—all prescribed forms of devotion, excepting those of Psalmody, are excluded, and every other part of the public service is conducted on the extemporaneous plan.

There was a period, indeed, when the practice of the Church of Scotland was different from what it now is, and has long been. In the earlier stages of her history, when, in emerging from the darkness and superstition of Popery, the number of pious and well qualified ministers was very small; and when, in the lack of regularly ordained men, it was deemed necessary sometimes to commit a portion of the public instruction to persons denominated *readers* and *exhorters*, it was found needful, in such cases, to provide some aid for the acceptable performance of public prayer. While the venerable John Knox lived, and for some time after his death, there was provision made for meeting this exigency by adopting at least a partial liturgy. Whether the liturgy thus adopted and used was the English liturgy of Edward VI, has been much disputed among the early historians of Scotland. As Knox was himself one of King Edward's chaplains; as he had been consulted respecting the liturgy sanctioned by that monarch; had found fault with it, and had procured its correction, to a certain extent, in accordance with his criticisms,[1] it is not at all unlikely that

[1] 'In the year 1551, Knox was consulted about the Book of Common Prayer (of England,) which was undergoing a revisal. On that occasion, it is probable that he was called up for a short time to London. Although the persons who had the chief direction of ecclesiastical affairs were not disposed, or did not deem it as yet expedient, to introduce that thorough reform which he judged necessary, in order to reduce the worship of the English Church to the Scripture model, his representations on this head were not altogether disregarded. He had influence to procure an important change in the communion office, completely excluding the notion of the corporeal presence of Christ in the sacrament, and guarding against the adoration of the elements, which was too much countenanced by the practice, still continued, of kneeling at their reception. In his 'Admonition to the Professors of the Truth in England,' Knox speaks of these amendments, as follows, with great apparent satisfaction: 'Also God gave boldness and knowledge to the court of Parliament to take away the round-clipped god, wherein standeth all the holiness of the Papists, and to command bread to be used at the Lord's Table, and to take away the most part of superstitions (kneeling at the Lord's table excepted,) which before profaned Christ's true religion.' These alterations gave great offence to the Papists. In a disputation with Latimer, after the accession of Queen Mary, the prolocutor, Dr Weston, complained of Knox's influence in procuring them. 'A runnagate Scot,' says he, 'did take away the adoration or worship of Christ in the Sacrament, by whose procurement that heresy was put into the last communion book: so much prevailed that one man's authority at that time.' In the following year he was employed in revising the Articles of Religion of the Church of England, previous to their ratification by Parliament.'— *M'Crie's Life of Knox*, p. 67. Strype questions the truth of Weston's statement, and says that Knox was hardly come into England, at least any further than New Castle, at

he favoured its partial and temporary use in Scotland. How long, or how extensively it was used is uncertain, and cannot now be decided. That all its forms were not adopted without exception we may take for granted. That liturgy appoints lessons to be read from the Apocrypha; but the Scottish Reformers expressly confined their public reading to the lessons of the Old and New Testaments. It is certain, that, as early as 1564, the Book of Common Order of Geneva, was in extensive use in the Church of Scotland, under the sanction of the General Assembly. But it is equally certain, that the prayers and other forms prescribed in that book were not intended to be throughout rigorously imposed on the conductors of public worship. It was, in fact, rather a 'Directory' for the worship of God, than a liturgy to be verbally and servilely repeated. In the Scottish Church, during the period in which this book was in use, the officiating minister was left at liberty to vary from it as he pleased, and to substitute prayers of his own in the room of those furnished in the book. The following quotations from the book will at once exemplify and confirm this statement: 'When the congregation is assembled at the hours appointed, the minister useth one of these two confessions, *or like in effect.*' Again: 'The minister after the sermon, useth this prayer following, *or such like.*' Similar declarations are prefixed to the prayers to be used at the celebration of Baptism, and the Lord's Supper. And at the end of the account of the public service of the Sabbath, this intimation is subjoined: 'It shall not be necessary for the

this time. Annals, iii. 117. But there is complete proof that he arrived in England in the beginning of 1549.—*M'Crie*, p. 68.

minister daily to repeat all these things before mentioned; but beginning with *some manner of confession*, to proceed to the sermon, which, ended, he either useth the prayer for all estates before mentioned, or else *prayeth as the Spirit of God shall move his heart*, framing the same according to the time and matter he hath entreated of.' And at the end of the form of excommunication, it is signified: 'This order may be enlarged or contracted, *as the wisdom of the discreet minister shall think expedient*. But we rather show the way to the ignorant, than prescribe order to the learned that cannot be amended.' The Scottish liturgy, then, was intended as a help to the ignorant, not as a restraint upon those who could pray without a set form. The 'readers' and 'exhorters' commonly used it; but even they were encouraged to perform the service in a different manner,[1] that is, to acquire the habit of praying extemporaneously to edification.[2]

This Directory, as it seems never to have been servilely recited by the most intelligent of the clergy, so it was soon laid aside. How long it was used is uncertain. As the clergy became more learned and more pious, it gradually fell into disuse.

Our chief concern at present is with those who regard liturgical forms of devotion, as not only highly desirable, but as even indispensable to a decent, edifying, and acceptable mode of conducting public prayer. In regard to such prescribed forms we shall endeavour to examine the arguments for and against them with as much impartiality

---

[1] Knox's Liturgy, pp. 83, 84, 86, 120, 189. Dunlop's Confessions.
[2] M'Crie's Life of Knox, pp. 432, 433.

and dispassionate respect to the reasonings of their friends, as possible.

And here, let it be distinctly understood, as a preliminary remark, that we are very far from pronouncing, or even thinking, that it is unlawful to conduct prayer, either public or private, by a form. We should deem such a sentence or opinion altogether erroneous. There is no reason to doubt that many a truly fervent and acceptable prayer has been offered in this manner. Some of the most excellent men that ever adorned the church of Christ have decisively preferred this method of conducting the devotions of the sanctuary; and have, no doubt, found it compatible with the most exalted spirit of prayer. We only contend, that such forms are not indispensable, as some contend, to orderly and edifying public prayer; that they are not equally edifying to all persons in all cases; that this is not, on the whole, the best mode of conducting the devotional services of the sanctuary; and, therefore, that to impose forms of prayer at all times, and upon all persons who publicly minister in holy things, and to confine them to the use of such forms, is by no means either desirable or wise. It is one of the main objects of the present volume, to impress upon the mind of every young Presbyterian minister who reads it, this sentiment, that while, on the one hand, the reading or recitation of prescribed prayers is by no means the best method of conducting the devotions of the sanctuary, and is liable to many weighty objections; so, on the other hand, it is a great mistake to imagine that sacred attention to the mode of conducting this service, and preparation for it can be safely neglected, or made the object of only occasional or superficial study; in short, that every Presbyterian minister who wishes to make the most of his services in the sanctuary, for the glory of God, and the best edification of his people, is bound to pay a greatly increased attention to the whole subject of public prayer.

In favour of constantly conducting the public devotions of the church by a prescribed liturgy, the following arguments have been commonly adduced.

I. It is alleged that public prayer under the Old Testament economy was always conducted by prescribed forms. This has been asserted, but never proved. And even if it were proved, it would by no means follow that a similar ritual ought to be used now. No one contends that all that was prescribed and obligatory under the Old Testament economy is still binding, or that the existence of any practice under that economy, makes it even lawful at present. Dr Prideaux, indeed, with many others, as mentioned in a preceding chapter, is very confident in maintaining the existence of liturgies under the old economy, not only in the temple, but also in the synagogue service. He gives, at length, what he calls the 'eighteen prayers,' prepared and used, as he contends, long before the coming of Christ.[1] But many of the best judges of Jewish antiquities consider that learned and laborious writer as having altogether failed to establish his position. And this has been the case with some of his own denomination, who, notwithstanding all their habits and preferences on the side of liturgies, have been constrained to believe that some of these 'eighteen prayers' bear internal proof of having been composed long after the

[1] Connection, Part i. Book vi.

coming of Christ.[1] Even in the temple service, for which so ample a provision of forms was furnished, there was no prescribed form of prayer; and even in the synagogue, or ordinary Sabbatical service of the later Jews, it has not been shown that they had any prescribed prayers, and far less that they were confined to them. If they had any such imposed forms, it is indeed wonderful that we do not find in all the inspired writings, in the works of Josephus or Philo, or in any other authentic writing, the least hint or allusion respecting them.

II. We are referred by the advocates of liturgies to that form or method of prayer which was given by the Saviour to his disciples, commonly called the Lord's Prayer, as presenting a plain, example of that for which they contend. The remarks made in the preceding chapter in regard to this prayer, it is not necessary here to repeat. But it is believed that every impartial reader will deem them quite sufficient to destroy the force of the whole plea drawn from this source, as an argument in favour of prescribed forms of prayer. If we do not find that prayer recorded in the same words by any two of the Evangelists; if it be adapted in its style and structure to the Old, rather than the New Testament dispensation; if it speak of the kingdom of God as not yet come; if it ask for nothing in the name of Christ, which was afterwards so strictly enjoined; if, after the resurrection and ascension of the Saviour, when the New Testament church was actually set up, we hear nothing more of this prayer as being at all in use in the apostolic age; surely all these considerations concur in proving that it could not

[1] Whitaker's Origin of Arianism, Chap. iv. Sect. ii. p. 302.

have been intended by the Master to enjoin it upon his disciples to be observed as an exact and permanent form.

Accordingly it is remarkable, as observed in the preceding chapter, that Augustine, in the fourth century, expresses the decisive opinion that Christ intended this prayer as a model rather than as a form; that he did not mean to teach his disciples what words they should use in prayer, but what things they should pray for; and understands it to be meant chiefly as a directory for secret and mental prayer, where words are not necessary.[1]

III. The advocates of liturgies assure us that such prescribed forms of prayer were used in the apostolic age, and that they have been constantly in use in the purest and most enlightened portions of the Christian church in all ages. But, unless I am greatly deceived, it has been demonstrated in the preceding chapter that no such statement can be made with truth; nay, that the contrary appears from all authentic history. It is indeed evident that in the early church the Christians had psalms and hymns, which they had adopted, and which they agreed in singing; that in administering baptism, and the sacramental supper, they were accustomed to employ the simple forms of administration found in the New Testament; and that in dismissing their worshipping assemblies, they were wont commonly to pronounce the apostolical benediction. But are there any regular churches on earth, even those which most entirely and confessedly exclude liturgies, which do not employ all the same auxiliaries in conducting the

[1] De Magistro, Cap. i.

service of the sanctuary? The Presbyterian Church has precisely all these; and yet is generally represented, and by some reproached, as having no liturgy. Indeed, would it be possible to unite in singing psalms or hymns without having them prepared and agreed upon before hand? Is it an evidence, then, either of good sense, or of candour, to employ the acknowledged use of forms in the psalmody of the early church as an argument in favour of prescribed, and against free prayer? But the simple and only proper question to be here decided, is, Had the Christian church, during the first five hundred years after Christ, prescribed forms of prayer, to which she was confined, or which she commonly employed in conducting her public devotions? How this question ought to be answered, has been shown, if I mistake not, conclusively in the preceding chapter.

IV. A further argument, frequently urged by the friends of liturgies against extemporary prayer, is, that it is difficult to follow anyone who does not pray by a form; indeed, that we cannot know whether we can join him in each successive sentence until the sentence is finished: so that we must be constantly kept in suspense until each petition is completed. This objection to extemporary prayer is chiefly imaginary. The difficulty which it represents as so formidable, is never really serious, and by habit is soon entirely overcome. Those who have complained of it at first, have acknowledged that, in a very little time, it ceased to incommode them. The operations of the mind are so rapid, that the moment a sober and scriptural petition is uttered, we can at once adopt it as our own. And, indeed, if free prayer be conducted in the best manner—that is, if it be founded on the matter and manner of the word of God, and abound in scriptural language, all who are familiar with the Bible can, of course, concur in and follow it without the least hesitation or embarrassment.

V. Another plea often urged in favour of established liturgies, is, that when constructed upon evangelical principles, they serve to perpetuate truth in the community by which they are used, and thus operate as a barrier against the inroads of error. We have the most palpable and undeniable evidence that this argument is far from being conclusive. There is, perhaps, no church in the world in which, for the last three hundred years, there has been a more constant use, and a more sovereign sway of their church service, than in the Church of England. But has her liturgy kept that church sound and pure, in accordance with the creed of those who formed it? Far from it. In that church, the number of the clergy and others who embrace and love the principles embodied in their articles and devotional forms, is comparatively small, probably amounting to much less than a quarter, or sixth part of the whole, and all manner of opinions, from the highest Calvinism to the lowest Socinianism, may be found among those who daily repeat and laud the same liturgy. What shall we say of the sovereign power of a liturgy as a barrier against error, when we find orthodox and evangelical men, and the most thoroughly Popish Puseyites that ever entered a sanctuary, repeating the same words every Sabbath with apparent cordiality?

But against those who employ this argument, the tables may be effectually turned. How often, nay, how much more frequently than otherwise, have the liturgical services of different churches served to countenance, extend, and perpetuate the most corrupt errors, and the most degrading superstitions! What have been the effects of the ecclesiastical formularies of the Romish Church, and of the various branches of the Greek and Oriental churches? Have *they* proved barriers against error? Have they not rather formed a sore bondage for extending and perpetuating corruption? What has been the effect of certain features in the liturgy of the Church of England; such as those which plainly imply and teach baptismal regeneration, and a number of other things savouring of Popish origin? Have not error and superstition been by these means countenanced, recommended, and established? Have not many enlightened and pious minds been grieved at the necessity laid upon them to repeat, in the presence of God, without the change of a word, these portions of their prescribed forms? And have not thousands wished in vain for an alteration in that which incontrolable authority compelled them *verbatim* to employ? What becomes of the preservative against error in such a case as this? True, the precious doctrines of the Trinity, of the divinity of Christ, of redemption through his atoning blood, and of justification by his righteousness, are so interwoven with that whole formulary, that no one can honestly use it who does not cordially believe in these great doctrines of the evangelical system. And yet how many hundreds have actually been in the habit of repeating it all their lives, who did not believe one word of any of these doctrines, and who were, of course, habitually guilty of that to which it is difficult, consistently with Christian courtesy, to give an appropriate name!

VI. The last plea in favour of prescribed forms of prayer which will be mentioned, is, that they only can effectually prevent those crude, inappropriate and revolting effusions which are so apt to characterize the public prayers of those who conduct them without a form. This is, in fact, the most plausible argument in the whole catalogue in favour of liturgies, and one which it becomes the friends of free prayer seriously to ponder in their minds, and to regard as a stimulus to attention and improvement. True, indeed, liturgical services themselves have sometimes been performed under circumstances, and in such a manner as to revolt every enlightened and tasteful mind. The annals of the church, if minutely examined, would furnish many such revolting examples. Still this fact does not justify the unseemly characteristics of extempore prayer wherever they occur. It cannot be denied, that this part of the service of the sanctuary has not commonly received that degree of attention, and been marked with that degree of excellence which ought to have been reached. The true remedy, however, is, not to have recourse to liturgies; but to apply to those means which will prepare to lead in public devotions in a fluent, appropriate, acceptable and edifying manner. We have seen what means Augustine recommended for correcting the faults of extempore prayer in his day; not to resort to liturgies, which had not been introduced; but to seek counsel and aid from the more experienced, pious and wise.

So much for the arguments usually adduced in favour of liturgies. Let us now turn to those considerations which satisfy Presbyterians that the liturgical plan of public worship is not the most eligible, and which lead them to a corresponding practice. And,

I. Why ought public prayers to be prescribed and imposed more than discourses from the pulpit? It is well known, indeed, that at an early period of the proceedings for reforming the Church of England, two books of 'Homilies,' or popular sermons, were actually prepared, and put into the hands of the officiating clergy to be read in order, and in rotation in all their pulpits. Yet I know not that even then ministers of acknowledged learning and talents were forbidden to compose and deliver such sermons as they thought proper to give. But why should restraint be exercised with regard to prayer, and not to preaching? If it be alleged that in prayer we speak to God, and, therefore, ought to exercise great reverence and consideration; is it not equally evident that in faithful gospel preaching, it is God speaking to us by his accredited servant; and that, of course, we ought to 'take heed' with no less attention, reverence, and awe, 'how and what we hear'? Why, then, is it more safe or more wise to permit ministers to preach as they please, than it is to allow them to pray as they please? If it be said, that the mass of ministers are now more enlightened and pious than they were when those formularies were composed for their use, the answer may be admitted; but it applies equally to the prayers as to the instructions of the sanctuary.

II. We are persuaded that liturgies have no countenance in the word of God, and were unknown in the primitive apostolic church; and, as Protestants, we feel bound to adopt and act upon the principle, that that which is not contained in Holy Scripture, or which cannot, by good and necessary consequence, be deduced from that which is contained in it, ought to have no place in the church of God. In reply to this argument, it has been strangely and weakly alleged, by those who have been constrained to yield to the force of historical testimony on this subject, that the only reason why liturgies were not used in the infancy of the church, was, that the enemies of Christianity were so numerous, and those who united in her worship were so very few, that there were none to make the necessary responses, and that it was judged better not to use prescribed forms at all than to use them imperfectly. Those who are capable of satisfying themselves with this subterfuge, forget that the preachers of the gospel, at the earliest period of their ministry, went forth, not alone, but 'two and two'; that scarcely any case can be imagined in which one or more auxiliary voices might not have been put in requisition; and that, if this mode of worship had been deemed by the great Head of the church not only most eligible, but so important to Christian edification as many of its advocates now deem it, nothing would have been more easy than for the omnipotent King of Zion so to order the affairs of his church, from the outset, as to open the way for its introduction. The truth is, however, that even in Jerusalem, where there were thousands of Christians, and in Antioch, where there were also many, and where, of course, responses would have been easy, we find no such practice recorded, or even hinted at. There was manifestly no such thing.

III. We not only find no evidence of any prescribed forms of prayer having been used in the apostolic age; but we do find testimony which plainly implies that no such forms were either prescribed or in use in the apostolic churches. If such forms had been established, where was the occasion, or even the propriety of Paul's exhorting Timothy to take care that 'prayers, intercessions, and giving of thanks be made for all men; for kings, and all in authority, that the people might lead quiet and peaceable lives in all godliness and honesty' (1 Tim. 2:1)? Can we suppose that liturgies had then been formed and established by the authority of inspired men? If so, had these subjects of petition been omitted in the prescribed formulary? This supposition would be strange indeed in regard to a liturgy formed by apostolic men. And if there had been no forms prescribed, how came it to pass that the apostle, in providing for the appropriate performance of this part of the service of the sanctuary, contented himself with giving a general 'directory,' rather than prescribing a precise form of words? Truly, it is impossible for an impartial mind to examine the New Testament without perceiving that it gives no countenance whatever to such a system of ritualism as that for which the zealous advocates of liturgies contend.

Prescribed forms of prayer appear to have been unknown in the Christian church for several hundred years after Christ. If the writer of these pages is not deceived, he has already produced ample proof of this. That testimony need not be repeated here. And indeed this fact is not denied by some of the most learned and zealous advocates of liturgical services. Now, that which had no place in the earliest, purest, and best periods of the history of the church, it surely cannot require much argument to show, is not essential to the edification of the body of Christ, and ought not to be considered as binding on his disciples. Some, indeed, have been so unreasonable as to contend, that, although no single public prayer was reduced to writing for the first four or five hundred years after Christ, yet much, if not the greater part, of the public prayer of that period was repeated from memory. This is a supposition as incredible as it is gratuitous. That which is delivered from memory is, of course, something previously composed. But where did those who committed to memory and repeated these prayers, obtain them? When, and by whom were they composed? Were they, as some dreamers imagine to have been the case with regard to the Homeric poems— floating in the popular mind for generations before they were committed to writing? If so, the difficulty is not yet solved. Was the church their original parent? or did they originate in some single 'master mind,' without the church's authority? If so, where is the evidence, on either supposition? Surely it is unreasonable, in a historical argument, to ask us to be satisfied with imagination or conjecture, instead of testimony.

But if, by alleging the early prayers to have been *memoriter*, be meant, that those who offered them, seldom uttered anything but that which they had either found in the Bible, or had heard from the wise and pious who had gone before them; it was probably even so, though there is absolutely no direct evidence to that amount in early Christian antiquity. But nothing can be more probable. That, however, is no argument against that prayer having been, throughout, extemporaneous. For there is probably no leader in extempore prayer at this hour who is often found to utter anything but what he has found in substance in sacred Scripture, or has heard, directly or indirectly, from the lips of some venerated father of the church.

IV. Confining ministers to forms of prayer in public worship tends to restrain and discourage both the spirit and the gift of prayer. The constant repetition of the same words, from year to year, is, undoubtedly, adapted, with multitudes of persons, to produce dullness and a loss of interest. We are very sure that it is so with not a few. Bishop Wilkins, though a firm friend to the use of liturgies, when needed, argues strongly against confining ourselves to such 'crutches,' as he emphatically calls them; and expresses the opinion, that giving vent to the desires and affections of the heart in extemporary prayer, is highly favourable to lively religious feeling and growth in grace. The following sentences are decisively expressive of this opinion. 'For anyone to sit down and satisfy himself with this book-prayer, or some prescript form, so as to go no further, this were still to remain in his infancy, and not to grow up into his new nature. This would be as if a man who had once need of crutches, should always afterwards make use of them, and so necessitate himself to a continual impotence. It is the duty of every Christian to grow and increase in all the parts of Christianity, as well gifts as graces; to exercise and improve every holy gift, and not to stifle any of those abilities wherewith God hath endowed them. Now, how can a man be said to live suitable to these rules who does not put forth himself in some attempts and endeavours of this kind? And, then, besides, how can a man suit his desires unto several emergencies? What one says of counsel to be had from books, may be fitly applied to this prayer by book; that it is commonly of itself something flat and dead, floating for the most part too much in generalities, and not particular enough for each several occasion. There is not that life and vigour in it, to engage the affections, as when it proceeds immediately from the soul itself, and is the natural expression of those particulars whereof we are most sensible.'[1]

The same opinion is also expressed by Bishop Hall, in a work written at a period when the subject of liturgies was discussed in his church with great learning and warmth, in which he delivers his opinion in the following decisive and pointed language.

'Far be it from me to dishearten any good Christian from the use of conceived prayer in his private devotions, and upon occasion also in public. I would hate to be guilty of pouring so much water on the spirit, to which I would gladly add oil rather. No, let the full soul freely pour out itself in gracious expressions of its holy thoughts into the bosom of the Almighty. Let both the sudden flashes of our quick ejaculations, and the constant flames of our more fixed conceptions, mount up from the altar of a zealous heart unto the throne of grace; and if there be some stops or solecisms in the fervent utterance of our private wants, these are so far from being offensive, that they are the most pleasing music in the ears of that God unto whom our prayers come. Let them be broken off with sighs and sobs, and incongruities of our delivery; our good God is

---

[1] Discourse concerning the Gift of Prayer, etc., chap. ii. pp. 9, 10.

no otherwise affected to this imperfect elocution than an indulgent parent is to the clipped and broken language of his dear child, which is more delightful to him than any other's smooth oratory. This is not to be opposed in another by any man that hath found the true operations of this grace in himself. What I have professed concerning conceived prayer, is that which I have ever allowed, ever practised, both in private and public. God is a free Spirit, and so should ours be in pouring out our voluntary devotions upon all occasions. Nothing hinders but that this liberty and a public liturgy should be good friends, and go hand in hand together; and whosoever would forcibly separate them, let them bear their own blame. The over vigorous pressing of the liturgy to the jostling out of preaching and of conceived prayer, never was intended either by the law makers or by the moderate governors of the church.'[1]

I have known persons who in early life were in the habitual use of extempory prayer, and who were then remarkably fervent and fluent in that exercise; but who, afterwards, from long confinement to forms, in a great measure lost the gift of extemporaneous prayer, and became embarrassed whenever they undertook to lead in social devotion. Examples of this might easily be selected, were it not inexpedient to detail personal anecdotes concerning men highly respectable for piety as well as intelligence, and on a subject too grave for ludicrous associations. We had republished in this country, a few years ago, a pamphlet entitled 'Scotch Presbyterian Eloquence Displayed,' in

---

[1] Humble Remonstrance for Liturgy and Episcopacy, and Defence of the Remonstrance.

which great pains were taken by a friend of liturgies to pour ridicule upon extemporaneous prayer by quoting, or feigning specimens of it from the mouths of Presbyterian ministers. It would not be difficult to produce an equally extended array of real cases in which Episcopal ministers, when cut off from the use of their prayer-books, have been perplexed and helpless to a deplorable degree.

It is said of the celebrated Bishop Patrick, that he had once remarkably excelled in free prayer; but that, toward the close of life, lodging at the house of a dissenter, with whom he had been long and affectionately intimate, he was requested to take the lead in family-worship, which he undertook; but was so much embarrassed, that he broke off in the midst of the prayer, arose from his knees, and apologized to his friend for his inability to proceed. His friend, perhaps more faithful than delicate, approaching him, said—'My friend, you have made a miserable exchange for your lawn sleeves and your mitre.' This anecdote is related, not for the purpose of depreciating the character of a truly eminent man, but to show, by a strong case, that, even a man possessing all the talents, learning, and piety, conceded to Bishop Patrick, if he ceases to exercise the gift of free prayer, will soon in a great measure lose it.

V. No prescribed forms of prayer, however ample or diversified, can be accommodated to all the circumstances, exigencies, and wants of either individual Christians, or a number of worshipping assemblies. Not only special dispensations of providence, and the continual changes going on in the church and the world; but the unceasing changes in the state of our own minds, can never be appropriately and fully expressed by any prescribed and immutable form. Now, when cases of this kind occur, which are not provided for in the prescribed form, what is to be done? Either extemporary prayer must be ventured upon, or the cases in question cannot be carried at all before the throne of grace.

A practical comment on this consideration was presented at the General Convention of the Protestant Episcopal Church in the United States, which met last year, (1847). One of the clerical members of that body, in the course of its proceedings, stated that, a short time before, a pious and grateful mother requested him to offer public thanks to God, on her behalf, for a signal domestic mercy. He was obliged, as he stated, to inform her, that the church had made no specific provision for returning thanks in such cases; and that he was not able to comply with her request. He, therefore, suggested, whether it would not be expedient to frame a new office adapted to such a case, and add it to the liturgy. His proposal was laid on the table, and eventually dismissed, on the distinct plea, that it was not desirable to favour *innovation*; that they had a liturgy venerable for its age, and sufficiently comprehensive for all desirable purposes; and that it was not wise to make provision in detail for such cases as that which he had proposed.

VI. It is no small argument against confining ministers and people to a prescribed form, that whenever religion is in a lively state in the heart of a minister accustomed to use a liturgy, and especially when it is powerfully revived among the members of his church, his form of prayer will seldom fail to be deemed more or less of a restraint, and liberty of free prayer to be desired. And this feeling will commonly either vent itself in fervent, extemporary prayer, or experience a sense of painful restraint under the prohibition; and perhaps be sensible of a diminution of spiritual life and enjoyment. The excellent Mr Baxter remarks, that 'a constant form is a certain way to bring the soul to a cold, insensible, formal worship.'[1] This language is by no means intended to assert, that there can be no real fervour of devotion where a form is constantly used, and even continued fervour to the end of life; but that strict confinement to such a form has a tendency to impair the warmth and the spirit of prayer; and that indulging the love of variety which is inherent in human nature, is friendly to vivid feeling, and heartfelt impression.

Besides, there are circumstances and situations in which a prescribed and often repeated form, however comprehensive and good, is not found to meet all the feelings and desires of a devout soul breathing after heaven. And hence there are moments when those who, both by conviction and habit, are most devoted to the use of liturgical forms, are willing to lay them aside. It is recorded of the celebrated Archbishop Secker, whose learning, talents, and warm attachment to the formularies of his church have been exceeded by few, that when he was confined to his bed by a broken limb, which ultimately terminated his life, he was visited at Lambeth by the Rev. Mr Talbot, a presbyter of his own church, who was remarkably pious, and who had long been on terms of great intimacy with him. The dying prelate said to him, in the course of the interview—'Talbot, you will

[1] Five Disputations, etc., p. 385.

pray with me'; and when he saw Mr Talbot rising to look for a prayer-book, he added 'That is not what I want *now*; kneel down by me, and pray for me in the way I know you are used to do.' The pious man did as he was requested. He poured out his heart in feeling and affectionate intercession for his illustrious friend, and took leave of him for the last time.[1]

VII. More than all this; there are exigencies in human life, in which the feeling heart is not only willing to lay aside prescribed forms as inadequate to the expression of our wants, but to turn away from them as in a great measure inapplicable. Let us figure to ourselves the situation of the large number of passengers who perished in the unfortunate steamer *Atlantic*, on the Long Island Sound, several years ago. The painful uncertainty, for a number of hours together, the protracted sufferings, and the final destruction of a large company of passengers, will not soon be forgotten by any who read the strong descriptions of that agonizing scene given at the time. Among the large number who met their death on that melancholy occasion, there were some truly pious people; some qualified and disposed to take refuge in the hopes and duties of religion. But what would have been their situation if, in the few broken opportunities for social prayer which were allowed them, they had been confined to liturgical forms? The very thought is revolting to the intelligent and pious mind. Surely the most servile admirers of such forms must see that something else was needed on such an occasion as this.

In like manner, let us contemplate the situation of a body

---

[1] Quoted by the Rev. Professor Porter, of Andover, in his Lectures on Homiletics.

of people like that of the inhabitants of Paris, a few months ago, when an enormous infuriated mob rose up against the government; when the whole country was agitated and alarmed; when thousands on both sides fell victims to the violence of civil war; and when, for four days together, the population of that great city knew not but that every house would be a scene of blood. It is to be feared that few, comparatively, of that agitated and infuriated mass had any disposition to pray, or any scriptural or intelligent views of a throne of grace. But what liturgy was ever adapted, or could possibly be adapted, to such a scene as that? Suppose the anxious, aching heart, occupied in pouring out all the fulness of its solicitudes, and all the urgency of its wants, at such a time, into the ears of the Lord of Sabaoth; or suppose a praying circle, in a retired street, if any street, at such a season, could be retired, and to have no other means of directing their petitions than the pages of a stated liturgy—what would be their feelings? Could they possibly regard the provision as either seasonable or satisfying? Could they, by means of such a form, cry to their covenant God, with the plenary utterance of the heart, as the people of God evidently did under the Old and the New Testament dispensations, when visited with special trials?

Take a single case more. Not long since, in one of the steamboats belonging to a passenger line between New York and Philadelphia, there was a young lady of respectable connections, and of highly interesting personal character, who, in the course of her passage on the Delaware, fell into the river, and was with great difficulty rescued from drowning. She was, however, finally taken from the water and brought back into the boat, in a state of entire insensibility. After half an hour spent in deep anxiety and distress respecting her, and in the laborious use of every restorative effort, animation was happily restored. When she regained her consciousness, a deep religious sentiment, for which she had long been remarkable, prompted her earnestly to beg those about her to unite in returning thanks to God for her happy deliverance. It was known that there was an Episcopal clergyman on board the boat; and he was requested to descend into the cabin, and to conduct such a service. He declined acceding to the request, on the plea that there was not in his prayer-book any office adapted to meet the case, or the expectations and wishes of the group who made the request. The consequence was, that a pious friend, who had been long accustomed to lead in extempore prayer, attended, and led the sympathizing, grateful circle in a most solemn and acceptable thanksgiving service.

If I know my own heart, I abhor the thought of employing the weapon of ridicule to the discredit of liturgical forms. It would be unreasonable to expect such forms to be provided for all supposable cases. But, in all sincerity and respectfulness, I must regard as essentially defective a system which, while it does not, and acknowledges that it cannot, provide for all cases which may arise, yet frowns upon all the prompt and voluntary provision which the dispensations of providence demand, and which heartfelt piety, and habitual communion with God, may be ready to furnish.

In the Church of England, when any great national calamity, or national blessing occurs, no minister of that church can publicly recognize it in prayer, until the ecclesiastical Primate thinks proper to move in the business, and to prepare and authorize an appropriate prayer for the occasion. How the Episcopal Church in this country would manage a similar occurrence, I know not. Would her ministers, with one accord, keep silence with regard to it in the reading-desk, until the next triennial convention should provide an adequate authority for framing and publishing a new form, or some bishop, or bench of bishops should 'take order' in the case? Would this be to enjoy that spiritual liberty with which Christ came to make his people free?

These and other allied considerations, satisfy me, beyond a doubt, that the claims of liturgies, as the best method of conducting our public devotions, and, above all, as the exclusive method, cannot be sustained. After carefully comparing the advantages and disadvantages of free and prescribed prayer, the argument, whether drawn from Scripture, from ecclesiastical history, or from Christian experience, is clearly in favour of the free or extemporary plan. True, indeed, its generally preferable and edifying character, may sometimes be marred by weak, or ignorant men; but we have no hesitation in saying that the balance is manifestly and greatly in its favour. As long as ministers of the gospel are educated and pious men, 'workmen that need not be ashamed,' qualified 'rightly to divide the word of truth,' and 'mighty in the Scriptures,' they will find no difficulty in conducting extemporary prayer to the honour of religion, and to the edification of the church. When they cease to possess this character, the case is undoubtedly altered. They then must have, and ought to have some aid provided for them. It was precisely in such a state of things—that is, when both intelligence and piety were declining—that the use of liturgies arose, and gradually crept into the church, as we have seen in a former chapter, in the fifth and sixth centuries after Christ. But it is manifestly the fault of ministers, if extempore prayer be not, what it may and ought ever to be, far more feeling and full of spiritual life and interest, than any imposed and often repeated form can be. Yes, it is the fault of the officiating minister in the Presbyterian Church, if prayer be not made the most tender, touching, and deeply impressive of all the services of the public sanctuary. When shall it thus be? May the Lord hasten it in his time!

The views of this subject taken by our venerated fathers, will appear from the following statement. The Liturgy of the Church of England was the prevailing, the almost universal formulary of public devotion in England up to the time when the Westminster Assembly of Divines was called together by the parliament, in 1643. There were individuals, indeed, who, anterior to that, considered the imposition of prescribed forms of prayer as unscriptural and by no means friendly to Christian edification; who thought that the Reformation in this respect had not been carried as far as it ought to have been: but still there were few individual ministers, and still fewer religious societies that dared to act upon this principle, and to indulge without restraint in their public assemblies, in extemporary prayer. In this state of the English nation, when the Assembly of divines came together, almost all of them having been episcopally ordained, and accustomed to the ritual of the established church, their prejudices and their old habits would, of course, naturally incline them, as far as they conscientiously could, to favour the old and established plan of worship. Accordingly, soon after the Assembly met, they received a message from the parliament, urging them to attend to the liturgy, and to report thereon to both houses of parliament 'with all convenient speed.'

Under this urgency, after some discussion, the Assembly agreed, by a large majority, to lay aside the use of all prescribed and imposed forms, and to report in favour of extemporary prayer. But, in order to avoid the imputation of opening the door too wide to irregular and undigested effusions in public worship, it was agreed to form and recommend to the parliament what was denominated a 'Directory for the Worship of God.' Against this plan for regulating the exercise of public prayer, the Independents, who formed a very small part of the Assembly, at first protested, as infringing the perfect liberty of prayer, which they thought desirable. They wished to leave the whole subject without regulation. Further discussion, however, reconciled the most, if not all of this party to the new plan, and the Directory at length passed the Assembly with great unanimity.

In reporting the Directory, as a plan intended to supersede the Liturgy, the Assembly offer the following reasons:

'It is evident,' say they, 'after long and sad experience, that the Liturgy used in the Church of England, notwithstanding the pains and the religious intentions of the compilers, has proved an offence to many of the godly at home, and to the reformed churches abroad. The enjoining the reading of all the prayers heightened the grievance; and the many unprofitable and burdensome ceremonies have occasioned much mischief, by disquieting the consciences of many who could not yield to them. Sundry good people have been kept by this means from the Lord's table, and many faithful ministers debarred from the exercise of their ministry, to the ruin of them and their families. The prelates and their faction have raised their estimation of it to such a height, as though God could be worshipped no other way but by the *service-book*; in consequence of which the preaching of the word has been depreciated, and, in some places, entirely neglected. In the meantime the Papists have made their advantage, this way, boasting that the Common Prayer Book came up to a compliance with a great part of their service; by which means they were not a little confirmed in their idolatry and superstition; especially of late, when new ceremonies were obtruded in the church daily. Besides, the liturgy has given great encouragement to an idle and unedifying ministry, who have chosen rather to confine themselves to forms made to their hands, than to exert themselves in the gift of prayer, with which our Saviour furnishes all those he calls to that office.

'For these and many other weighty considerations, relating to the book in general, besides divers particulars which are a just ground of offence, it is thought advisable to set aside the former liturgy, with the many rites and ceremonies formerly used in the worship of God; not out of any affectation of novelty, nor with any intention to disparage our first Reformers, but that we may answer, in some measure, the gracious providence of God, which now calls upon us for a further reformation; that we may satisfy our own consciences; answer the expectations of other Reformed churches; ease the consciences of many godly persons among ourselves, and give a public testimony of our endeavours after an uniformity in divine worship, pursuant to what we have promised.'[1]

Nor did these views originate in the Westminster Assembly, or in the men of that generation. Three quarters of a century before that Assembly met, some of the most pious and learned men in England, and not a few of them dignitaries of the church, spoke the same language. While they did not deny the lawfulness of using set forms of prayer, they complained of being *confined* to them, and earnestly petitioned for the privilege of using extemporary prayer both before and after sermon. They also complained of responses in prayer, as having no foundation in the word of God, or in the purest ages of antiquity. But their complaints were disregarded, and their petitions met with no favour.

[1] See Neal's History of the Puritans, Vol. ii. 106, quarto edition.

CHAPTER 4

FREQUENT FAULTS OF PUBLIC PRAYER

IN all the exercises of the pulpit, mannerism is apt, on all sides, to creep in; that is, certain favourite thoughts, illustrations, or modes of expression are apt to obtrude themselves more frequently than occasion demands, or than good taste allows. Such thoughts or expressions may become, if often repeated, highly offensive to pious and cultivated worshippers. This is more especially the case, if they be repugnant to either good grammar or good sense. These are of various kinds, and have, of course, very different degrees of offensiveness. It is the province of good sense and of good taste to avoid them. And it is surely incumbent upon all who are called to officiate in the service in question, to be unceasingly on the watch to guard against everything adapted to inflict pain, or interfere with the edification of a single mind.

It is far from being my aim to encourage that spirit of excessive refinement, that fastidious intolerance of minor blemishes in the devotions of the sanctuary which is sometimes manifested by those who care much more about the taste of the external ceremonies, than about the life and power of religion. I would earnestly deprecate the indulgence of such a spirit in the house of God. It ought to be as much as possible banished from our public assemblies. Still, while we caution serious minds against being too much revolted even by real blemishes in the mode of conducting public devotion, we ought not to hide from ourselves that they are blemishes, which it is far better to avoid than to defend.

The faults which I have in view are as various as they are multiplied. I shall merely specify a few; others will readily occur to enlightened and vigilant observers.

I. In the first place, a very common fault is the over frequent recurrence of favourite words, and set forms of expression, however unexceptionable in themselves. Among these are the constant repetition in every sentence or two, of the names and titles of God; the perpetual recurrence of the modes of expression, '*O God!—great God!—our heavenly Father!—holy Father!*'—'*we pray thee*'—'*we beseech thee*'—'*we entreat thee to grant,*' etc., or the excessive use of the interjection *Oh!* prefixed to almost every sentence. With many, these appear to be mere expletives; with others, they seem to furnish a kind of resting place for the mind, to afford an opportunity for reflecting on what is to follow; and hence they have been called the 'setting poles' of preaching and prayer. In all they fill up a space which might be better occupied by coming directly to the object itself prayed for. Besides, this incessant repetition of particular words or phrases, renders them cheap, and, after a time, not merely superfluous, but disgusting—a feeling which ought to be as much as possible banished from every devotional exercise. Nay, there is something in this matter more serious still.

If the constant repetition of the name of the Most High, even in prayer, be not 'taking the name of the Lord our God in vain,' it certainly approaches very near to that sin. We are sometimes called to join in prayers in which that holy name occurs in almost every sentence from the beginning to the end.

II. Hesitation and apparent embarrassment in utterance, is another fault of very frequent occurrence, and a real blemish in the leader in public devotion. As all prayer is to be regarded as the utterance of the heart, so the suppliant ought to be supposed to be at no loss, to have no hesitation about the blessing which he solicits. When, therefore, he pauses, stumbles, recalls, or goes back to correct, he unavoidably gives pain to every fellow worshipper, and always leaves the impression of a mind less intent, a heart less fervently engaged, than it ought to be. All stammering, then, all pauses, all recalling or exchanging words, all want of proper fluency; in short, everything adapted to impair, for a moment, the confidence of fellow worshippers in the ability of him who leads, to get on with entire ease, comfort, and success, ought to be deemed real faults, and to be as much as possible avoided.

III. All ungrammatical expressions in prayer—all expressions foreign from English idiom, and bordering on the style of cant and whining, low and colloquial phrases, etc., ought, of course, to be regarded as blemishes, and to be carefully avoided. These are by no means so uncommon as might be supposed. Even educated men, by inadvertence, by strange habit, by various unaccountable means, are betrayed into faults of this kind, and are sometimes found to adhere to them with wonderful obstinacy. Of these there will be an attempt to give a small specimen only. It is no uncommon thing to hear ministers, who, in other respects, are entitled to the character of correct speakers, say, 'Grant to *give* us the sanctifying power of the Holy Spirit'; '*Grant* to impart to us the consolations of thy grace'; 'Come down in our *midst*'; '*Make one* in our *midst*'; '*Lay us out* for thyself'; 'We commit *us* to thee'; 'We resign *us* into thy hands'; '*Solemnize* our minds.' These, and many similar expressions, are among the minor instances, which too often occur, of forgetfulness of English idiom, and of strict grammatical rules. The more gross offences against both are passed over here, as too revolting to be recited, and as not to be corrected by cursory hints, but by a return to radical instruction. True, indeed, where there is much of the 'spirit of prayer,' much of that faith and love and elevated devotion which belong to the 'fervent, effectual prayer of the righteous man,' we ought not to indulge, as before remarked, in too much fastidiousness in regard to language. Yet, while it is admitted that the formality of carefully adjusted rhetoric ought to have no place in either secret or social prayer; while 'the enticing words of man's wisdom' ought not to be sought in the cry of sinners for pardoning mercy and sanctifying grace—still, he who undertakes to be the leader and helper of others in their devotions, ought to remember that he is a debtor to the wise, as well as the unwise, to the learned as well as the illiterate; that there are numbers in every congregation, who, though they have no taste for piety, have some claim to literary culture; and, therefore, that it is incumbent on him to be qualified to perform his work in such a manner as shall not be revolting to the most cultivated of those whose mouth he is at the throne of grace. In this, as well as in every other part of spiritual service, it is important to 'find out acceptable words.' It is evident, from a passage in a former chapter, that in the days of the learned and pious Augustine there were some, who, in their public prayers, fell into barbarisms and solecisms, in regard to which the venerable father cautions those to whom he wrote, against being offended at such expressions, because God does not regard the language employed so much as the state of the heart, and he, at the same time, exhorts those who fell into these faults, to employ the appropriate means, which he prescribes, for avoiding them in future.

IV. The want of *regularity* and *order* is a fault which frequently and greatly impairs the acceptable and edifying character of public prayers. All public prayer which bears the comprehensive character which belongs to that exercise, is made up of various departments; such as adoration, confession, thanksgiving, petition, and intercession. A public prayer which should be entirely destitute of any one of these departments, would be deemed essentially defective; and a prayer in which these several departments should all be so mixed up together throughout the whole as that they should all go on together in this state of confused mixture, from the beginning to the end, would, doubtless, be considered as very ill judged and untasteful in its structure; nay, as adapted essentially to interfere with the edification of intelligent worshippers. Not that the *same order* should always be maintained. This would be a serious fault of an opposite kind. It is the absence of all order that is here meant to be censured, and represented as a fault.

V. Descending to too much *minuteness of detail* in particular departments of prayer, is another fault of unhappy influence in this part of the public service. As a well conducted public prayer ought to consist of many parts, so it is evident that the undue protraction of any one or more of these parts, must of necessity lead either to inordinate length in the whole exercise, or to the omission of other parts equally important. Not only so, but this minuteness of detail may be carried so far as to become revolting in itself to the mind of every intelligent worshipper. It is proper, no doubt, to return thanks to God for the fruits of the earth, especially on days set apart for public thanksgiving. But suppose the leader in such a service, instead of contenting himself with grateful general acknowledgments for the products of the soil, and a favourable and abundant harvest, furnishing food for man and beast, should think himself called upon to descend to such minuteness of detail as to specify by name all the various kinds of grain, and all the productions of the garden, the field and the meadow, specifying those which were deemed of most importance, and which had been yielded in the greatest abundance, would he be deemed wise and judicious? Would it not be much better to content himself with acknowledging the goodness of God in sending a fruitful season, and an abundant harvest, providing abundance of food for all who stood in need of it? In like manner, if a neighbourhood had been visited with severe and mortal sickness of various kinds, it surely would not be proper, in a prayer in which it was intended to acknowledge the righteous judgment of God in the case, and to humble ourselves under his mighty hand, to recount by name all the forms of disease which had proved distressing or fatal, referring to the various proportions in which they had respectively prevailed. It would be quite enough to speak in general of prevailing sickness and mortality, to acknowledge the hand of God in the dispensation, to pray for the sanctified use of all his dealings, and to implore his sustaining and consoling grace for all those families which he had been pleased to bereave. I have sometimes known the dignified and solemn nature of the exercise greatly impaired by descending to particulars to a degree bordering on the ludicrous, and by no means favourable to pure and elevated devotion. I once knew a minister who, in making a prayer at the funeral of an aged patriarch, who left a large family of children, went over, by name, all the sons and daughters of the family, alluding graphically to the character and situation of each, some being quite unfavourable. I also knew another, who, during our revolutionary war, in alluding, in a public prayer, to a sanguinary battle which had been recently fought, gave a detailed account of the killed and wounded on both sides, and all the leading circumstances of the conflict.

VI. Closely connected with this fault in public prayer is another, of which we often hear serious complaint. It is that of *excessive length*. This is so common and so crying a fault that it ought to be mentioned with emphasis, and guarded against with special care. The state of the mind in right prayer is one of the most elevated and interesting in which it can be placed. Of course, such is the weakness of our faculties, and their tendency to flag, that an exercise of this fervent and exalted character ought not to be long continued. The leader himself cannot always keep up the full tide of spiritual feeling, for any length of time together; and even if *he* could, those who unite with him in worship may not be always equally successful. Hence, what is more common, in looking over our religious assemblies in time of prayer, than to see one half of the worshippers, after a short time, grow weary of the standing posture, and sitting down for relief? This may indeed be done, and often is done, without reason, and very improperly; but it is unhappy to furnish even a pretext for it. An ordinary prayer before sermon, ought not to exceed twelve, or at most fifteen minutes in length. All protraction of the exercise beyond that length does not help, but rather hinders devotion. Some allowance indeed, as to this point ought to be made for days of special prayer, either of thanksgiving, or of humiliation and fasting; for as prayer ought to form a larger element than common in the exercises of such days, so, of course, more time for it ought to be allowed; so that, on such occasions, several minutes more may with propriety be added to the devotional parts of the service. But, after all allowance for extra cases, the excessive length of public prayers still remains a crying grievance: and it appears impossible in some cases to make the offenders sensible of their fault. It is not meant by this that the leader in public prayer should pray *by the clock*; but that he should, by habit, which any thinking observant man may easily form, learn to guard against that inconsiderate tedious-ness which soon banishes all devotion. The celebrated Mr

Whitefield, after being greatly fatigued with preaching one evening, requested the father of the family in whose house he lodged, to conduct the domestic worship before retiring to rest. The pious gentleman protracted his family prayer so inordinately that Mr Whitefield, in the midst of it, rose from his knees, sat in his chair and groaned audibly; and when it was ended, he took his friend by the hand, and said with strong feeling, 'Brother, how can you allow yourself to indulge such tediousness in your domestic devotions? You prayed me *into* a delightful frame of mind, and you prayed me completely *out* of it again.'

VII. An abundant use of highly figurative language, is another blemish in public prayer, of which we sometimes find examples. All studied refinement of language; all artificial structure of sentences; all affectation of the beauties of rhetoric, are out of place in the exercise of right prayer. Both evangelical solemnity, and good taste equally forbid them. Here many offend. Even the eloquent and evangelical Dr Jay, of Bath, in England, in his published volume of prayers has not wholly avoided this fault. His devotional language in too many cases lacks the unaffected simplicity which ought to characterize it. It has too little of the language of Scripture. It is artificial, rhetorical, elaborate, abounding unduly in ornate and studied forms of speech, in point, antithesis and other rhetorical figures. This is often beautiful. Some greatly admire it and call it an eloquent prayer. But the fervent utterance of the heart is always simple. Here laboured rhetorical language is out of taste, and out of place. They are surely in great error, then, who seem to aim continually to clothe their petitions in public in high-sounding language, with elaborate ingenuity; who are constantly recurring to language drawn from the thunder, the earthquake, the ocean, the splendour of the solar beams, the mighty flood, the lofty mountain, etc., etc. I once knew an eloquent and eminently popular preacher, who seemed to aim at concentrating in his prayers all the bold, high-sounding, sublime thoughts and figures which he could collect from the natural and moral worlds; so that he seemed to be ever upon a kind of descriptive stilts, and exerting himself to exhibit on every subject this rhetorical grandeur. He succeeded in gaining the admiration of multitudes, but was not equally acceptable to the more simple-hearted and devout of those to whom he ministered.

I have even known some preachers, not unfrequently, in public prayer to quote lines of poetry, and in a few cases, the greater part of a striking, beautiful stanza. To be very fond of making such quotations in sermons, is not in the best taste; but to do it in prayer, is certainly a much graver offence against the dictates of sound judgment.

VIII. It is a serious fault in public prayer to introduce allusions to *party politics*, and especially to indulge in *personalities*. As the minister of the gospel who leads in public prayer is, as it were, the mouth of hundreds, and sometimes of thousands, in addressing the throne of grace, he ought not, if he can consistently with duty avoid it, to introduce into this exercise anything that has a tendency to agitate, to produce secular resentment, or unnecessary offence of any kind in the minds of any portion of the worshippers. In the house of God persons of all political opinions may meet, harmoniously and affectionately meet, provided they all agree in acknowledging the same Saviour, and glorying in the same hope of divine mercy. They may differ endlessly in their political creeds and wishes, and on a thousand other subjects, and yet assemble in the same temple, and gather round the same altar with fraternal affection, provided they are of one heart, and of one way in regard to the great system of salvation through the redemption that is in Christ. Why, then, should the feelings of brethren in Christ be invaded in their approaches to the throne of grace by unnecessary allusions to points in which the strongest worldly feelings are painfully embarked? It is impolitic. It is cruel. It often presents a most serious obstacle to the success of the gospel. It has a thousand times produced distraction and division in churches before united, and constrained many to separate themselves from their appropriate places of worship, and from all the means of grace.

Having been myself betrayed in early life, on various occasions, into a course of conduct in relation to this matter which was afterwards regretted, I resolved, more than thirty years ago, never to allow myself, either in public prayer or preaching, to utter a syllable, in periods of great political excitement and party strife, that would enable any human being so much as to conjecture to which side in the political conflict I leaned. This has been my aim; and this is my judgment still: and this course, unless in very extraordinary cases, which must furnish a law for themselves, I would earnestly recommend to every minister of the gospel. The more those who minister in holy things are abstracted from political conflicts, even in common conversation, and much more in their public work, the better. They have infinitely more important work to do than to lend their agency to the unhallowed conflicts of political partisans. 'Let the dead bury their dead.'

No less unsuitable and unhappy is the influence of all personalities in public prayer. All praying *at* people; all recognition of the private scandal of the week in the devotions of the house of God; all allusions to the private injuries or griefs which he who officiates has recently received; all singling out conspicuous individuals in a neighbourhood, and holding them up to public view in our petitions, whether for commendation or censure: everything of this kind is improper in its nature and mischievous in its influence—adapted to excite various unhallowed feelings in the house of God, and to drive individuals from the sanctuary.

On this subject I would say, that even when prayers are requested for the family, or in any respect for the benefit of persons who are supposed to be present in the assembly, we may go too much into detail—too far in holding them up personally to view, or indulging in language complimentary to their standing or importance in society. In regard to points of this sort it is always better to err on the side of reserve and brevity than the reverse.

IX. All expressions of the *amatory class* ought to be sedulously avoided in the public devotions of the house of God. Those who lead in prayer are sometimes unhappily betrayed into language of this kind. We sometimes, though not very frequently, hear those who are fervent and importunate in prayer, use such expressions as—'dear Jesus'—'sweet Jesus'—'lovely Saviour,' and various other terms of a similar class. All such language, though flowing from earnestness, and dictated by the best of motives, is unhappy, and produces on the minds of the judicious painful impressions.

X. The practice of indulging in *wit*, *humour*, or *sarcasm* in public prayer, is highly objectionable, and ought never to be allowed. This, though not often, is sometimes witnessed, and, perhaps we may say, especially by men of powerful minds, and strong feelings, and who are accustomed, on that account, to feel that they may 'take liberties' in their public ministrations. A small specimen of what is intended here will be sufficient.

It being once intimated to a popular clergyman, who was strongly opposed to the administration of President Jefferson, that his omitting to pray for the president, in his public devotions had been remarked with regret, he came out on the following Sabbath, in his prayer, with a reference to the subject, in something like the following brief and pointed style:—'Lord, look with thy favour upon our public rulers. Bless the President of the United States. Give him wisdom to discharge his important duties aright; for thou knowest he *exceedingly needs it.*' Another popular preacher, eminently a man of wit, warmly opposed to the administration of the then President, on a day of public humiliation, fasting, and prayer to which the United States had been called by the President's proclamation, expressed himself in public prayer as follows: 'Almighty God, who sittest as governor among the nations, and who rulest over all! we have been called by our chief magistrate to humble ourselves before thee, and to ask for thy gracious interposition in our behalf;

but thou knowest he has not called us to this duty, until by his unwise administration he had brought us into a condition which renders aid from above peculiarly desirable and necessary; for vain is the help of man.' One more example shall suffice. An excellent clergyman, of powerful mind and strong feelings, having been deeply impressed by a recent instance of parsimony on the part of a church toward her pastor, in consequence of which his health and comfort had been seriously impaired, prayed, at a church meeting, in the following strain:—'Almighty King of Zion, guard and sustain thine own cause. Protect and strengthen thy ministering servants. Have mercy upon such of thy professing people as have no compassion on labourers in the gospel field, and who seem to be desirous of making the experiment whether they can most speedily destroy their lives by overworking or by starving them.'

It is earnestly to be hoped that such examples will not be considered as proper for imitation. If they be not profane in their spirit, they are certainly much more adapted to promote profane than devout feelings. I should expect a general smile to pervade an assembly on the utterance of such petitions. There are those who call praying in this style, fidelity; but it is often the product of a very different spirit, and will be generally avoided by those who wish to utter the truth with the 'meekness of wisdom.' If any minister of the gospel has wit or sarcasm, or anything of like character, on his mind, of which he wishes to be delivered, as a stroke at any person or cause, it is most earnestly to be desired that he will seek some other channel for giving it vent than the public prayers of the sanctuary.

XI. The excellence of a public prayer may be marred by introducing into it a large portion of didactic statement, and, either in the language of Scripture, or any other language, laying down formal exhibitions of Christian doctrine. It will be seen, in the next chapter, that the devout recognition of fundamental doctrine in prayer is an excellence, and ought ever to make a part of it; but this ought always to be presented in a devotional form, and ought never to wear the aspect of a theological lecture addressed to him who sits on a throne of grace. This fault, however, will be sufficiently guarded against in a future chapter. In the meanwhile, it should be recognized as a real fault, and care taken to avoid every approach to it, that may be adapted to give pain to an intelligent worshipper.

XII. Another fault nearly allied to this is worthy of notice. I have known a few persons who were not only in the habit of introducing into their public prayers abundant didactic statement of doctrine; but who also seemed studious of introducing, with much point, those doctrines which are most offensive to the carnal heart, and which seldom fail to be revolting to our impenitent hearers. We Presbyterians profess to preach a system of doctrine, some of the parts of which, especially those which recognize the absolute sovereignty of God in the dispensation of his grace, all unsanctified men of course hate, and which, whenever they are announced, excite uncomfortable feelings and opposition among the great mass of mankind. Still, we are bound to preach these doctrines, whether men will hear, or whether they will forbear. These doctrines were preached by the inspired apostles. They were offensive to a great majority of those to whom they were delivered, and it is so to the present hour. Yet, we are not to preach them continually, and to the exclusion of everything else; but, as the apostles did, in proper order, in proper connection, and in wise measure. To be fond of introducing them in prayer, argues a mind not cast in the apostolic mould, and inordinately set on partial views of truth.

XIII. Too great *familiarity* of language in addressing the High and Holy One, is also revolting to pious minds, and ought to be sacredly avoided. There are those who, on the principle of indulging in filial confidence, and a strong faith, address God as they would speak to an equal—claiming the fulfilment of his promises—insisting on the bestowment of what they wish—and, in short, employing, without scruple, the language of earthly and carnal urgency. This is not in accordance with that deep humility, that profound reverence, and solemn awe with which suppliants, conscious of unworthiness, ought ever to approach the infinite majesty of heaven and earth. The filial, but humble confidence of a dutiful child, is one thing; the presumptuous familiarity of one who thinks much more of his own wishes and will than of his deep unworthiness as a sinner, and of the infinite holiness and majesty of the Being to whom his prayer is addressed, is quite another. There is such a thing as appearing at home before the mercy-seat, and pleading with God with all the freedom and confidence of an affectionate child; and there is also such a thing as, under the guise of prayer, 'speaking unadvisedly with our lips,' and forgetting that even the heavens are not clean in the sight of him who sits on the throne of grace.

XIV. Further; there is such a thing as expressing *unseasonably*, and also as carrying to an *extreme* the professions of humility. The former is sometimes exemplified, by ministers of the gospel, in praying for themselves in the public assembly. Often have I heard ministers in leading the public devotions of the sanctuary, pray for divine assistance in preaching the word. This is very proper, and may be so expressed as to be at once delicate, acceptable and edifying. But suppose the petition on this subject to be expressed in some such manner as this, which I have actually and repeatedly heard: 'Lord, assist thy servant, one of the most weak and unworthy of men, a very child in spiritual things, in attempting to open and apply the Scriptures,' etc. And again, 'Help him, in all his weakness and ignorance, rightly to divide the word of truth, and to give to each a portion in due season.' Such language might be altogether unexceptionable in secret prayer, in which, if the humble petitioner really and honestly made this estimate of himself, he might with great propriety express it before the Lord. But when he addresses God as the mouth of hundreds of worshippers, there is surely no propriety in putting into the mouths of all his fellow suppliants, language concerning himself which he would consider as indelicate and offensive if employed by one of them in praying for him. Suppose he should hear one of his elders or deacons pray for him in similar language, and say, 'Lord, help our minister in preaching for us today. Thou knowest that he is one of the weakest and most unworthy of men; thou knowest he is but a child in spiritual things, and needs thy help in the discharge of every duty.' Would he consider this as becoming language in the mouth of another concerning himself? How then can he reconcile it with propriety to put language into the mouths of hundreds concerning his own character which he would consider as unsuitable if uttered by any one of them? Whatever, then, any man might be willing to say of himself in his closet, let him never utter anything in prayer in the pulpit respecting himself, which he would not be willing that any and every person should say of him in similar circumstances.

In regard to expressions of extreme humility in public prayer, we may also find examples. It is not common, indeed, nor is it easy to take a lower place before the mercy-seat than our demerit as sinners justifies. And yet I think language on this subject has sometimes been employed which a sound judgment and a correct taste ought to have forbidden. To exemplify my meaning. A warm-hearted and eminently pious minister of our church, on the occasion of a meeting of one of our Synods, when the Lord's Supper was dispensed, and when it was customary in that ordinance, to employ a number of successive tables; the first table being filled entirely with ministers; in the course of the prayer, setting apart the elements, he expressed himself thus: 'O Lord, thou knowest we are most unworthy. Thou knowest there was never gathered round a sacramental table a more polluted, unworthy set of sinners than those who are now seated before thee.' The good man undoubtedly meant to recognize the idea that to whomsoever much was given, of them should much be required; and that the sins of ministers, in opposition to their light and their vows and obligations, were to be regarded as inferring more guilt than those of other men. But when he ventured to say in prayer, that no band of communicants was ever more corrupt and vile than those which surrounded that table, the probability is that he went beyond the truth, and, with a good meaning, was chargeable with indulging in pious, certainly in unseasonable extravagance.

XV. Again; everything approaching to *flattery* is a serious fault in public prayer, and ought to be carefully avoided. Flattery in any man and on any occasion is criminal. In the pulpit it is eminently so: but to convey anything like flattery in prayer, is undoubtedly liable to still heavier censure. Yet, something nearly resembling this, not infrequently occurs in the public devotions of the sanctuary. I refer to the language often employed in prayer after a brother in the ministry has preached, or performed some other equivalent service. That prayer is often employed as a vehicle of strong commendation, not to say flattery of the preceding preacher. It is by no means uncommon, in this part of the public service, for him who performs it to express himself in some such language as the following: 'We thank thee, O Lord, for the interesting, the solemn, and the truly scriptural discourse to which we have just listened'; or,—'We pray that the richly instructive, powerful and excellent discourse which thy servant has just given us, may sink down into our hearts.' And on some rare occasions, thanks are returned that 'such a burning and shining light has been raised up'; and a petition offered, 'that he may shine with increasing lustre as he advances in years'; and that 'his departure, like the setting sun, may be serene and full of glory.' In short, with many preachers, the closing prayer, in all such cases is considered as furnishing a kind of theological thermometer, by which we may graduate the warmth or the coldness of the approbation felt for the sermon which has just closed.

This ill judged and very exceptionable practice has become, with many preachers, so common, that if one should omit to convey, in some form, the usual compliment, he is by some considered as wanting in civility, and as manifesting a want of respect to the preacher. And although persons of sound judgment and good taste generally avoid this impropriety; yet, as might be expected, the more injudicious and indiscreet are most apt to launch out in language of warm eulogy, and, through this devotional medium, to pay compliments altogether unmerited, and if ever so much merited, altogether unseasonable.

It would, indeed, be over fastidious to forbid, in a closing prayer, any reference to a preceding preacher. To pray that the word as delivered by him may be accompanied with the Holy Ghost sent down from heaven; that it may prove like good seed sown in good ground, and bring forth abundant fruit to the glory of God; and that the preacher may be graciously rewarded for his labour of love, and may see the work of the Lord prospering under his ministrations—may undoubtedly be allowed without offence, nay, without impropriety. But nothing that savours of compliment, direct or indirect, either to the talents or the piety of the preacher, is, in any ordinary case, allowable. And certainly, it is in all cases, safest and best to err on the side of reserve and abstinence than of excess.

There is a tradition that the following circumstances once occurred in the life of the elder President Edwards.

He had engaged to preach on a certain Sabbath for a neighbouring pastor. When the day arrived, the pastor went to his pulpit at the appointed time, but did not find Mr Edwards there. He waited as long as he thought proper, and Mr Edwards still not appearing, he began the service. In the course of the prayer which usually precedes the sermon, Mr Edwards, who had been retarded by an unexpected occurrence, entered the church; and, being remarkably gentle and quiet in all his movements, he came into the house, made his way to the pulpit, and placed himself by the side of the pastor without being observed. The pastor, in his prayer, taking for granted that Mr Edwards was still absent, had allowed himself to express regret that he had failed to come, and that the congregation was to be disappointed: he also launched out in expressions of profound respect for the talents, learning and piety of Mr Edwards, thanking God that he had raised up so eminent an instrument for doing good, and that he had been enabled to accomplish so much by his learned and able works; and praying that his important life might be spared, and his usefulness extended to the remotest parts of the land. At the close of his prayer, to his astonishment, he found Mr Edwards standing by his side, and ready to perform the service which had been expected of him. With some little embarrassment he said, 'Sir, I did not know that you were present; if I had known it, I should not have prayed as I did.' But feeling as if it might do good to throw into the scale something to balance his compliments, he added—'But after all, they do say that your wife has more piety than you.'

XVI. The *want of appropriateness*, is another fault often chargeable on public prayer. In some rare cases, we find ministers who excel in this branch of the worship of the sanctuary, whose topics and language are all dictated by the occasion on which they officiate. From beginning to end they are appropriate. The intelligent fellow worshipper recognizes a fitness, an adaptedness in every petition, and in every sentence. Without any apparent study or effort, everything seems to be in keeping with the occasion which has brought them together, and the scene before them. This is a great excellence, and never fails to make a happy impression on pious and enlightened worshippers. But with how many who officiate in public prayer is it far otherwise! If they are called to conduct this exercise on the first day of the year; on a day of humiliation and fasting, or of thanksgiving; at the visitation of a Sabbath School; at the opening of a judicatory of the church; at the dispensation of a sacrament; or at the ordination of a minister, the greater part of the petitions they utter would be equally applicable to any other service or occasion. Perhaps an eighth, or a tenth part only of what they utter can be considered as applicable to the occasion before them, or as entirely seasonable. I once knew a member of one of our presbyteries, who, when called upon to make the ordaining prayer, at the solemnity of setting apart a minister to the sacred office, went back to the beginning of time; traced the progress of civil and ecclesiastical society; alluded to the various plans of electing and ordaining the officers of the church all along down through the patriarchal and ceremonial dispensations; and, at length, after tiring out every worshipper with the tediousness of his deduction, he came to the New Testament dispensation, and made about one-quarter part of his inordinately long prayer really adapted to the occasion on which he was called to officiate. During a large part of the time occupied by this prayer he had his hands, as well as the hands of his fellow presbyters, pressing on the head of the candidate to the great discomfort of all.

I have heard it stated as a remarkable excellence in the late Doctor Emmons, of Massachusetts, that in all his public prayers he was so peculiarly appropriate, that, while he was richly various and judicious, every petition, from the first sentence to the last, was strictly adapted to the occasion on which he was called to preside. There is a singular beauty in this, and a direct tendency to increase the interest and the edification of the exercise; while the obvious effect of the opposite course is to exhaust the patience, and fatigue the attention before coming to that which really belongs to the occasion.

XVII. Another fault in public prayer, which I have often observed and regretted, is, the apparent want of *reverence* with which it is frequently concluded. It is not easy intelligibly to describe this, in many cases. The thing referred to, is an air and manner, and especially a tone of voice, indicating not only a purpose and desire to close, but some degree of haste to be done, manifested by pronouncing the last sentence or two with more rapidity, in a less solemn tone, with less fervour and apparent earnestness than the preceding. Nay, I have known some occupants of the pulpit, to all appearance, decisively pious, who, on closing a solemn prayer of otherwise excellent character throughout, have not only uttered the last sentence in the hasty and irreverent manner just described, but they have been seen, while pronouncing the last sentence, stretching forth their hands and grasping the psalm book, that they might be ready, without the loss of a moment, to give out the psalm or hymn that followed.

There is something not a little revolting in all this. Surely he who leads in a solemn prayer ought to be at least as seriously and earnestly engaged as any other individual in the sanctuary. But what would he think if the whole assembly, or any considerable portion of them, were observed to be engaged, during the last sentences of his prayer in adjusting their dress, or in putting in their appropriate places all the fixtures around them? Surely such a sight would fill him with disgust, and would call forth a pointed rebuke. Of all persons present, the officiating minister ought to manifest the most exemplary sincerity and earnestness in uttering every sentence of his own devotions, and, to the last word, to exhibit an attention fixed, a solemnity undiminished and complete.

XVIII. The last fault in public prayer that will be here mentioned, is that *rapidity* and *vehemence* of utterance, which are sometimes affected as an expression of deep feeling, and ardent importunity. This rapidity is oftentimes carried so far as to be inconsistent with that calm reverence which is essential in all addresses to the infinitely exalted object of prayer. Here nothing hasty, nothing rash, nothing which has not been considered and weighed, ought ever to escape from the lips of him who leads others to the throne of grace. There is hardly anything more attractive and impressive in this exercise than the appearance of a sanctified intelligence, as well as a warm heart, dictating and accompanying every petition; when there is an opportunity given for him who leads, as well as for him who follows, to reflect well on what is uttered; to begin no sentence without forecasting its import and its conclusion; and thus to avoid that sudden embarrassment which is often the result of inconsiderate haste. How revolting to hear him who is the mouth, perhaps, of hundreds, in addressing the High and Holy One, pouring out his petitions with such vehemence, such extreme rapidity, such a blast of voice, as to give those who are listening to him no opportunity to ponder in their hearts what he is saying, and to unite in heart with him! He who gives himself up to this kind of headlong speed of manner, will often fail of carrying along with him the intelligent concurrence of his fellow worshippers, and will be apt to stumble in his hasty progress, from not having well considered what he is about to say. Words 'few,' 'well considered,' and 'well ordered,' are the inspired characteristics of a good prayer.

In fact, in this exercise the whole manner is important and worthy of being sacredly regarded. Here, all unnecessary vociferation; all stern, ostentatious, disrespectful, dictatorial tones of voice; everything not in keeping with that modest, humble, filial spirit which becomes a suppliant conscious of deep unworthiness, and pleading for mercy, ought to be carefully avoided; nay, a right frame of mind will ever spontaneously lead to their avoidance.

I once knew a young minister who, in common conversation, was remarkably gentle and deliberate; and in preaching rather below than above par in ardour and animation; but who, as soon as he commenced the exercise of prayer, became rapid, impetuous, and even boisterous. The consequence was, that he hurried on at a rate which prevented many from keeping up with him; that he began sentences without foreseeing how they were to end; that he stumbled and blundered, and sometimes excited the disgust rather than the devotion of the assembly.

I am sensible that, while I have given this formidable list of faults which frequently occur in public extempore prayer, it would be an easy thing to present an equally extended array of faults which I have heard of, or observed on the part of those who recited liturgies. The truth is, where good sense, good taste, and fervent piety are not in exercise, no public office of devotion can be really well performed. But it is no part of my plan to turn other denominations into ridicule, or to dwell on the faults of our neighbours. This would give me no pleasure. Nor would it in the least degree mitigate my pain in contemplating the faults which exist among ourselves. I submit to the pain of mentioning the faults which sometimes occur in our own beloved church, if haply I may minister to their removal, or the diminution of their number. God forbid that I should ever intrude into another Christian denomination for the sake of wounding feelings. I would much rather look at home, and 'cast the beam out of our own eye,' that we may 'see clearly to cast the mote out of our brother's eye.'

CHAPTER 5

CHARACTERISTICS OF A GOOD PUBLIC PRAYER

O N this subject the enlightened and pious heart is the best human guide. Yet even piety, however ardent, and talent and knowledge, however mature, may not be above the need, or beyond the reach of some general counsels which experience may suggest. An attempt will be made to offer a few suggestions, which, however superfluous with regard to many, may not be so in respect to all. And here I shall, of course, omit many of those characteristics of a good prayer which are to be taken for granted as always indispensable—as that it be sincere— that it be offered in faith—in the name of Christ—with deep humility—with firm reliance on the Saviour—with submission—with confidence in a pardoning God, etc. All these are to be taken for granted as essential in every acceptable prayer. But some considerations which are apt to be forgotten claim our special notice, and occupy, in my judgment, an important place in the list of counsels. And,

I. One of the most essential excellencies in public prayer, and that which I feel constrained first of all, and above all to recommend, is, *that it abound in the language of the word of God.*

This characteristic in all social addresses to the throne of grace is recommended by a variety of considerations.

(1.) This language is always right, always safe, and always edifying. Whatever doubts we may have concerning other language, in regard to this there can be none. It silences all objection, terminates all cavil.

(2.) There is in the language of the sacred Scriptures a simplicity, a tenderness, a touching eloquence peculiarly adapted to engage and impress the heart. Among all the stores of human diction, there is nothing so well fitted to take hold of the mind as that which we have been accustomed from our infancy to read in the inspired pages, and, by association, to connect with all that is solemn in eternal things, and with all that is interesting in the hopes of the soul. Even worldly men, of mere literary taste, have agreed in pronouncing the Bible to be the great storehouse of that language which is better adapted than any other to impress the popular mind, and to take hold of the best feelings of the soul.

(3.) It has been often suggested by the advocates of liturgies, that it is not easy for them to follow a leader in extemporary prayer, because they cannot know the full extent of any petition until the sentence embracing it is completed; so that they are constantly held, they tell us, in a kind of suspense, until each successive sentence is terminated, uncertain whether they can make the prayer their own until each part of it, in succession, is fully uttered. I have known some warm friends of prescribed forms of prayer, who acknowledged that this difficulty was much diminished, and, indeed, in a great measure removed, when they became accustomed to extemporaneous prayer: but still they complained of it as, for a time, a real inconvenience. Now this objection would have no place, or, at least, none worth mentioning, if the leader in public prayer made a point of deriving a large part of his petitions and his general diction from the word of God. He would carry with him in every successive sentence, the unhesitating concurrence, and the entire approbation of every fellow worshipper. Nay, the concurrence and the approbation would be yielded in advance the moment the well known language, the beloved and venerated phraseology of the sacred oracles sounded in the ear.

On these accounts it is, that many judicious Christians lament the absence of this feature in not a few of the prayers of some modern preachers, otherwise of no small excellence. Where the mind of the minister is deeply imbued with the language and spirit of the word of God, there is, surely, no occasion in which this ought to be more manifest, and more richly and tenderly employed, than in his acts of devotion; and where it is thus manifested, there is nothing more calculated to fall with pleasure and with profit both on the ear and the heart of every intelligent hearer.

But in incorporating the language of Scripture with our public prayers, there may be great and unhappy mistakes in various ways. It is not every part even of the Bible, that is well suited to be repeated in addressing the throne of grace. Passages of Scripture not at all devotional in their form, but rather didactic or historical, may be, and often have been incorporated with prayer in such a manner as to disturb and not aid the feelings appropriate to that exercise.

A minister called to officiate at an ordination, quoted in his prayer that passage which is found in 1 Tim. 3:1-4: 'This is a true saying, if a man desire the office of a bishop, he desireth a good work. A bishop, then, must be blameless, the husband of one wife, vigilant, sober, of good behaviour, given to hospitality, apt to teach; not given to wine; no striker, not greedy of filthy lucre; but patient; not a brawler, not covetous; one that ruleth well his own house, having his children in subjection with all gravity.' Thus he went on, quoting the simple didactic passage, without any attempt to throw the substance of it, as, with a little ingenuity, he might have done, into a devotional form; and seemed to think he had done well because he employed the language of the Bible.

In like manner, another, in his public prayer introduced the last two verses of Romans 2 thus: 'For he is not a Jew which is one outwardly; neither is that circumcision which is outward in the flesh; but he is a Jew which is one inwardly; and circumcision is that of the heart, in the spirit, and not in the letter; whose praise is not of men, but of God.'

This is what many have called 'preaching in prayer.' And, truly, this quaint title is by no means inapplicable.

But there may be, and sometimes has been a still more revolting use of the language of Scripture in prayer. I refer to cases in which passages of the word of God bordering on the ludicrous, or the indelicate, have been unscrupulously incorporated with the exercise of public prayer. I once knew an excellent man, of fervent piety, and of strong good sense, whom I have heard, not once only, but many times, in deploring the torpor and unfruitfulness of the church, and praying for a revival of religion, to say, in allusion to the tree planted in a vineyard, which brought forth no fruit—'Lord, we deserve thy righteous judgments; we bring forth no fruit as we ought—but O let us not be deprived of the privileges which we have so criminally failed of improving—cut us not down; but dig about us, *dung us*, and make us to bring forth fruit to the glory of thy holy name.'

Another, equally unscrupulous, provided he used the language of Scripture, did not hesitate to quote in his prayer the expression of the Psalmist, in the seventy-third Psalm. 'They that are far from thee shall perish. Thou wilt destroy all them that go a whoring from thee.' Surely we are not driven by any scarcity of more eligible texts, to select these for incorporating with our devotional addresses to the Majesty of Heaven. The Bible is so full of passages, not only rich and appropriate in their spiritual meaning, but also directly and tenderly devotional in their whole scope and structure, that it appears to be a strange taste indeed, that would fasten on portions of the inspired volume, which, though inserted by holy men as they were moved by the Holy Ghost, and strictly in place as a part of the sacred narrative, are by no means adapted to edify a mixed assembly in the devotions of the pulpit.

Again: language found in Scripture may not be entirely adapted to modern use, because founded on topography, or usages no longer intelligible to common minds. Ministers, in praying for the spread of the gospel, have often been heard to quote or allude to a passage in Zechariah 9:10. May his dominion extend 'from sea to sea, and from the river to the ends of the earth.' In adopting this quotation, what river is meant? To an inhabitant of Palestine, three thousand years ago, it was, no doubt, intelligible and significant; but what distinct idea does it convey to a worshipper in Great Britain or the United States? So the passage which occurs in Psalm 121:1: 'I will lift up my eyes unto the hills, from whence cometh my help,' is not infrequently repeated in prayer. But what is the idea which it conveys to common minds? Jerusalem was built upon a mountain, and Judea was a mountainous country, and the Jews, in their several dispersions, turned towards Jerusalem when they offered up their prayers to God. But no such idea is conveyed to the popular ear among us, when this Scripture is quoted.

I once knew an excellent minister, long since deceased, who appeared to me to judge erroneously on this subject in another way, less exceptionable, indeed, but worthy of notice. His prayer always consisted purely of passages of Scripture strung together, without anything of his own. In fact it was, almost without exception, from beginning to end, an uninterrupted chain of Scripture texts, without any other links than those which the texts themselves formed. This looked so much like the studied utterance of the memory rather than of the heart, that I remember to have listened to him, and united with him, with less pleasure than with others, who were not so much the mere repeaters of texts of Scripture from the beginning to the end of their prayers; as constantly guided by the spirit of the Bible, and referring abundantly to its diction, but not entirely or servilely confined to either. This easy, natural, unstudied mode of employing Scripture in public prayer, is adapted to please and edify all, without exciting the idea of study or formality in any.

II. Another excellence of a good public prayer is, that it be *orderly*. That is, that it have a real and perceptible order. Not that it be characterized by formality; not that it be always in the same order; but still that its several parts of adoration, confession, thanksgiving, petition and intercession, should not be jumbled together in careless, inconsiderate mixture; but made to succeed each other in some happy arrangement. A fault in regard to this point was noticed at some length in a preceding chapter. But some reference to the positive advantages resulting from a proper attention to it, may not be out of place here.

Regular order has a good effect on him who leads in prayer. It presents regular landmarks, which assist his memory, and prevent the omission of any important part of the exercise. It furnishes a very essential element in enabling him to judge of the length of his prayers; and it diffuses a kind of light over his whole progress in the duty, which cannot fail to exert a happy influence on his own mind.

A good and tasteful order in prayer has also a tendency to operate favourably on the minds of all the worshippers who join in it. When the leader mingles together all the several parts of prayer, so that his fellow worshippers are constantly interrupted by his passing from one to another without warning, and without order, it breaks in on the flow of appropriate feeling; so that when the mind is in some measure prepared to indulge in a devout flow of feeling, something comes in to change the current, before it has time to take effect, and make the appropriate and profitable impression. This cannot fail of producing an effect equally unfriendly to comfort and to edification.

An adherence to order in prayer is likewise favourable, as before hinted, to the proper length of the exercise. Where no arrangement is adopted; where the several topics are regulated by no plan of succession; the leader has less perception, than if it were otherwise, of the passage of time. He lacks one of the best means of judging of the length of his own prayers, and is more apt, on that account, to be insensible of the progress of time, and to become uncomfortably tedious.

But this counsel will be greatly misapprehended, if it be supposed that the same order ought always to be observed. This would lead to objectionable formality. It is, doubtless, better continually to vary the order, and thus to relieve the minds of the worshippers from the tedium of constant sameness. Sometimes confession of sin and unworthiness may, with propriety, hold the first place in this exercise. At other times, it may be proper to begin with thanksgiving; and in like manner to diversify the order of the other departments of prayer. In early life it was my privilege often to be a witness of the ministrations in the pulpit of the late President Dwight, whose learning, piety and taste were so conspicuous in the estimation of all who knew him. His public prayers were uncommonly rich, copious, and interesting. But he continually altered their arrangement; and confined himself to no one order. I have known him, when he officiated more than once in the same pulpit on the same day, not only to diversify, with unlimited freedom, the order of his topics, but also to pass by some of them, at one time, with slight notice, and, at another, to dwell upon them much more in detail. I remember to have observed, on one occasion, that he in a great measure omitted in his prayer, in the forenoon, that part usually called intercession, which, in the afternoon, shortening other parts to accommodate his purpose, he took up and enlarged upon, in a very striking and edifying manner. And there can be no doubt, that a sound judgment and good taste will often dictate, when we are called to officiate in prayer on special occasions, that we are not only at liberty, but required by every principle of seasonable propriety, to vary our order, and while we shorten or omit some parts, enlarge on others, to which the occasion may seem specially to call our attention.

III. A suitable prayer in the public assembly is dignified and general in its plan, and comprehensive in its requests, without descending to too much detail. This was noticed in a preceding chapter, but is worthy of a repeated suggestion. In secret prayer there is no objection to the most minute particularity. When alone with God, we may without impropriety, dwell with unlimited enlargement and importunity on whatever occupies our hearts, or is deemed desirable for our interest. We find examples in Scripture of pious people spending hours together in importunate prayer for special mercies. But in public prayer, as the exercise ought not to be protracted, in ordinary cases, as before remarked, beyond the space of twelve, or at most, fifteen minutes, so our topics ought to be of that general character which may be considered as applicable to the whole assembly. Particularity may be carried so far as not to meet the feelings of the mass of the worshippers, and sometimes to an extreme, as hinted in a former chapter, which borders on the ludicrous. Everything of this kind ought to be avoided; and while that false dignity which aims at stately and formal generalities alone, ought never to be indulged; yet the opposite extreme is by no means adapted to minister to the edification of intelligent Christians.

IV. A good public prayer should be carefully guarded, in all its parts, against *undue prolixity*. The fault of excessive length in this part of the public service has been so emphatically censured in the preceding chapter, that there is the less need of enlarging directly on this point in the present connection. But it has sometimes escaped notice that one of the most essential means of avoiding excessive length, is not only to avoid multiplying topics unnecessarily and excessively, but also to avoid undue enlargement on the topics which are selected as the subjects of petition. A fault here is exceedingly common. Many a prayer has been unhappily protracted by not only selecting too many topics, but also by indulging in inexpedient dilation and diffuseness on the several topics. There is often an inconsiderate and ill-judged profusion of words, and substantial if not verbal repetition in this exercise which ought to be avoided. It is in prayer especially important that our words be 'few,' as well as 'well ordered.'

It is not meant, indeed, to be denied that on special occasions, those parts of a prayer which are appropriate to the occasion may be, and ought to be more extended than the rest. But then, in order to avoid transcending due limits as to time, the other parts ought, in all such cases, to be proportionally shortened, that the whole may not become too long. It is really worth some management and pains to avoid that fatiguing prolixity which is so often found to interfere with edification.

It is no excuse, as many seem to think, for excessive length in prayer, that they cannot, in a shorter time embrace every object of which they wish to take notice. This is apologizing for one fault by pleading for the necessity of another. It is better to pass over some topics in a cursory manner, or to omit them altogether, rather than to induce weariness in a single pious worshipper. There is no more need of including everything that is appropriate and desirable in the same prayer, than there is of embracing everything that belongs to a given text in the same sermon. If we yielded, in the latter case, instead of spending thirty-five or forty minutes in our ordinary discourses, we should seldom be able to get through in less than two hours. The fact is, it ought to be our aim in prayer, as well as in preaching, to leave off before weariness approaches, and in that full tide of elevated feeling which becomes the later as well as the earlier stages of that solemn exercise. The venerable and learned Cotton Mather speaks of it as a great accomplishment in a young preacher, more than a century ago, that he could pray a whole hour in public without the least repetition. I trust no one whose eye meets this page will be inclined to emulate such an accomplishment.

V. Another excellence of a public prayer is, that it be *seasonable*, and *appropriate* to the occasion on which it is uttered. There is a great beauty in this, and a happy impression resulting from it whenever it occurs. The prayers recorded in Scripture, for the most part, bear this character in a very striking manner. Almost all of them are, from beginning to end, strictly appropriate, and would not have been really suitable on any other occasions than those on which they were actually delivered. There is something very trying to the judgment, as well as the patience of the intelligent worshipper, when he who leads in prayer has a long, preliminary, and inapplicable series of topics on which he dwells to the point of weariness, before he comes to those which belong to the occasion on which he officiates. This is exceedingly unwise. Whether it be done in the pulpit, in the missionary meeting, in administering a sacrament, in the Sabbath-school, or in the sick room, it is ill-judged and unhappy in its influence.

Another important advantage of an adherence to perfect appropriateness in public prayer is, that it is one of the best means of guarding against excessive and unseasonable length. Almost all the undue prolixity which we observe and lament in this exercise, is referable to a defect here. When he who leads in prayer does not confine himself to that which belongs to the occasion on which he officiates, he is liable to be borne away by his feelings, or by his want of self-possession, into any extent of irrelevant matter, and, of course, may be betrayed, before he is aware, into the most undesirable tediousness; whereas he who carefully adheres to that which is appropriate to the occasion, will find himself furnished with the best of all guards against every indulgence in tedious prolixity.

VI. It is an important excellence in a public prayer, that it include the recognition of so much *gospel truth*, as to be richly instructive to all who join in it, as well as all who

listen to it. Truth is the food of the soul. Gospel truth is that
on which the Christian lives and grows from day to day.
And, although it is rather the design of preaching than of
prayer to convey didactic instruction to our hearers; and
although, as stated in a preceding chapter, the practice of
'preaching in prayer' is really a serious fault, and ought to
be sacredly avoided, yet it cannot have escaped the notice
of any intelligent attendant on the service of the sanctuary,
that much doctrinal instruction may be and is continually
incorporated with almost all the public prayers recorded
in the sacred volume. Who does not see that, in all those
prayers, the great doctrines of our entire dependence on
God; our utter unworthiness of his favour; our apostasy and
corruption as children of the first Adam; our recovery by the
incarnation and atoning sacrifice of the second Adam, the
Lord from heaven; the necessity of our renewal by the Holy
Spirit, and of our justification by the imputed righteousness
of Christ, and our entire indebtedness to his grace for
every holy desire and action: who, I say, does not know
that all these doctrines are directly or indirectly implied,
and shine forth in many of the devotional compositions
found in the sacred pages? And who does not know that
when we arise to address the throne of grace, as the mouth
of few or of many, we have not only the fairest opportunity
of directing the minds of our fellow worshippers to these
great truths, and of endeavouring to fasten their attention
upon them as the life of the soul; but that they must, if we
would pray aright, be devoutly interwoven through all our
addresses to the God of mercy? Nay, I have sometimes
thought that if a wise physician of the soul were searching

for the most insinuating and impressive medium through which to address either a Christian or a worldly man, on the great truths of the gospel, he could seldom find any so well adapted to his purpose as wise, discriminating, tender prayer; a prayer comprehending thought, and a seasonable, pointed, forcible exhibition of truth. We are told that Mr Whitefield often conveyed to his hearers, of various characters, through the medium of happily directed prayer, alternately the most tender and affectionate counsel, the most withering rebuke, and the most pointed instruction that ever escaped his lips.

Of course, in public and social prayer, Christian doctrine is rather implied and intimated than directly and formally laid down. Yet nothing can be plainer than that a skilful conductor of public devotion has one of the very best opportunities for inculcating divine truth, in the most touching and impressive of all connections. It is a great part of practical wisdom, then, in those who are called to preside in prayer, either with the sick or the well; either in the private circle, or the public assembly—to introduce as much precious truth into their prayers as they possibly can without falling into a didactic strain; as much as is consistent with that simple, filial, suppliant character which ought to pervade all our devotional exercises.

VII. Another important feature of great excellence in public prayer, is *a desirable degree of variety*. We object to being confined to prescribed forms of prayer, because they lay us under the necessity of repeating not only the same topics, but also the same words in public devotions from year to year. But I have known Presbyterian ministers whose public prayers were so much alike for years together, that one of their fellow worshippers long accustomed to their ministrations, might with confidence go before them every Sabbath, and anticipate all that they had to utter in this exercise. This is a great evil, so entirely at variance with our professed principles, so much adapted in our view, to interfere with edification, and so adverse to continued attention on the part of those who worship with us, that it surely deserves the attention of all who are called to preside in this important part of the public service. Truly it is with an ill grace that some of our ministers find fault with the sameness of liturgies, when their own prayers have as much of this quality as any that we hear read, with the disadvantage of being decidedly inferior both in matter and manner.

But the study of variety may be carried to an extreme. I once heard of a minister of our church so scrupulously careful as to this point, that he resolved never, if he could possibly avoid it, to utter a second time, a single sentence that he had ever before uttered. This was, no doubt, an extravagant zeal for variety, and adapted to beget a censurable scrupulosity, rather than a truly devout spirit. But while we fly from this unprofitable extreme, it is surely worth while to take appropriate pains to attain that happy variety, which can only be acquired by taking measures to bring out of our treasure, in this respect, as well as in preaching, 'things new and old.'

VIII. Almost all ministers close their prayers with a *doxology*, copied more or less closely, from the sacred oracles. This is a plain dictate of Christian principle, and directly warranted by revealed examples. But are ministers as careful as the Bible is to vary these doxologies? It strikes me that there is a great beauty in doing so, and that it is greatly adapted to gratify the pious heart. Sometimes the closing doxology in prayer is repeated thus: 'To the Father, to the Son, and to the Holy Ghost be glory for ever. Amen!' Sometimes thus: 'Now unto him that is able to keep us from falling, and to present us faultless before the presence of his glory with exceeding joy: to the only wise God our Saviour, be glory and majesty, dominion and power, both now and ever. Amen!' And sometimes: 'To God the Father, Son, and Holy Spirit, be all honour and glory now and ever! Amen!' It would minister, it seems to me, to an increase of interest in our public prayers, if these and other various forms were adopted more frequently, than they are. They might be alternated and applied in a manner adapted to rouse the feelings, and warm the hearts of worshippers who are less impressed by the constant use of only one doxology. I have often doubted whether, with regard to this point, a sufficiently rousing and animating variety is habitually consulted. I once heard of a minister who, in a time of revival, when his own heart, as well as the hearts of his hearers were unusually warmed with the power of the Holy Spirit, closed a prayer in the midst of the revival, with great acceptance, and with strong impression, in the words of the Psalmist, (Psa. 72:18, 19): 'Blessed be the Lord God, the God of Israel, who only doeth wondrous things; and blessed be his glorious name for ever; and let the whole earth be filled with his glory. Amen! and Amen!' The effect was electric in suddenness, and most happy.

IX. A good public prayer ought always to include a strongly marked reference to, *the spread of the gospel*, and earnest petitions for the success of the means employed by the church for that purpose. As it forms a large part of the duty of the church to spread the knowledge of the way of salvation to all around her, and to send it, to the utmost of her power, to all within her reach who are destitute of it; so she ought never to assemble without recognizing this obligation, and fervently praying for grace and strength to fulfil it. So prominent an object in the church's duty ought, undoubtedly, to form an equally prominent object in her desires and prayers. Were petitions on this subject made to occupy the place, and to wear the aspect which they ought to do, it would tend to keep this great duty constantly before the mind of the pastor himself, and before the minds of all his people, in something of its appropriate and solemn character. That duty which was thus solemnly acknowledged and prayed over every Sabbath, could hardly fail to occupy the attention and to impress the hearts of those who adhere to this practice. We seldom, indeed, hear a public prayer which wholly omits all reference to the spread of the gospel. But O how often is the reference to it the most cursory and chilling imaginable; without point, without apparent engagedness; neither manifesting interest on the part of the minister, nor adapted to beget interest in his fellow worshippers! No wonder that in churches in which this is the character of the public prayers we hear of few and stinted contributions to the great missionary cause. If this cause were carried into the pulpit every Lord's day, and there presented before the Lord in the distinct, solemn—and touching manner which its importance demands, we surely should not find so many of the churches on our roll so entirely delinquent in regard to this duty, as our records annually disclose.

X. Another consideration worthy of notice here is *the manner in which the Most High is addressed* in different parts of public prayer. It is common for those who officiate in this solemn exercise, to adopt some one title of God, which they carry, for the most part, through the whole prayer. Whether it be that of 'Almighty God,' or 'Heavenly Father,' or any other favourite title, it is repeated and hackneyed, whatever may be the burden of the confession, the grateful acknowledgment, or the importunate petition. How much more appropriate, and in accordance with a spiritual taste, would it be, frequently to alter this title, as we pass from one part of prayer to another, adverting all along to the extent, the diversity, and the glory of the divine attributes! Thus, suppose a prayer for the revival, the prosperity, and the enlargement of the church, were prefaced with the following appeal—'O thou Sovereign King of Zion, who hast purchased her with thine own blood, and hast given to her exceeding great and precious promises, look upon thine own feeble, struggling church in mercy. Wilt thou not revive her, that thy people may rejoice in thee? Wilt thou not lift her from the dust, and clothe her in beauty, through thine own comeliness put upon her? Wilt thou not cause her, amidst all her darkness, to look forth clear as the sun, fair as the moon, and terrible as an army with banners?'

Again; suppose prayer were about to be made for the dispersion of popular ignorance, and the diffusion of the light of science, and above all, of the light of life in Christ Jesus our Lord, among all classes of men;—and suppose the suitable petitions on that subject were introduced thus: 'O thou Source of all knowledge, with whom there is light, and no darkness at all, have mercy upon our land. Thou alone art able to scatter the shades of night that rest upon the nations. Send, we beseech thee, far and wide, the light of science, and especially the light of the glorious gospel of the blessed God, to all people from the rising to the setting sun. Let our children, and the children of all around us, be trained up in the nurture and admonition of the Lord, and let all kindreds and people and nations and tongues be made to know thee the only true God, and Jesus Christ whom thou hast sent.' And so, if we were about to pray for the speedy and extended conversion of impenitent men, we might enter on the topic in some such way as the following: 'O thou who delightest not in the death of the sinner, but rather that he turn unto thee and live, have compassion upon those who know thee not, and will not have thee to reign over them. Open their eyes before it be for ever too late; convince them of sin, and bring them willingly to the love, the service, and the glory of him, who, though he was rich, yet for our sakes became poor, that we through his poverty might be rich.'

These appropriate titles, and modes of addressing the Most High, are not only in perfect keeping with the petitions intended to follow them; but they are adapted to prepare the minds of worshippers for uniting in those petitions, and for giving them a more prompt and edifying access to their feelings. I cannot help thinking that this plan would recommend itself to the Christian judgment of many, if it were once fairly and largely adopted.

XI. A good public prayer *should ever be strongly marked with the spirit and the language of hope and confidence.* Strictly speaking, it is the church alone that really prays. If so, her prayers ought ever to be couched in the language of filial love, and of humble, tender reliance on the favour and faithfulness of her covenant God. The devout, heavenly-minded M'Cheyne, states, in one of his familiar letters, that a certain pious minister had remarked concerning the prayers of another minister, that he prayed 'as if he thought that God was not willing to grant the blessings which he asked.' It is a real fault when prayers wear an aspect in accordance with this remark. Our gracious covenant God loves to be taken at his word; to be firmly and affectionately trusted; to have his exceeding great and precious promises importunately pleaded; and to be approached as a willing, tender Father, not only 'mighty to save,' but ready and willing to save; more ready to bestow the gifts of his grace than earthly parents to give good things to their children. This is, perhaps, the true idea of the 'prayer of faith'; and the more strongly it marks all our approaches to the throne of grace, the more is it in accordance with the spirit of the covenant of grace.

XII. The *prayer after sermon*, which is commonly short, is very often, not only a brief, but a mere general, pointless, and uninteresting effusion, simply imploring a divine blessing on what has been said, equally applicable to every similar occasion, and only adapted to prepare the way for the close of the service. Instead of this, the closing prayer ought to be framed upon the plan of making it, as far as possible, one of the most solemn, appropriate, and impressive parts of the whole service. It ought to be formed upon the plan of taking hold of the conscience and the heart most deeply and effectually, and of uniting as far as possible the most pointed and searching solemnity of application, with the most perfect tenderness and affection of appeal. The closing prayers of Whitefield were often peculiarly appropriate and inimitably touching; and those of Nettleton were, perhaps, never exceeded for appropriate simplicity, and adaptedness to seal the impressions of the preceding sermon. The preacher who can consent, after delivering a sermon of solemn, discriminating character, to close, as is often done, with a few sentences of perfectly common-place prayer, as much adapted to one subject as another, is guilty of abandoning an advantage which ought to be dear to a wise man. Every sentence of the prayer after sermon ought to be thoughtfully and carefully constructed upon the plan of deepening and riveting every impression attempted to be made in the preceding discourse. And, for this purpose, it ought to be, on common occasions, rather longer than it usually is, and constructed upon a principle of rich appropriateness in following the sermon.

XIII. In regard to the use of *the Lord's Prayer* in the devotions of the sanctuary, it is proper, in this chapter, to make some remarks. It has been seen, I trust, in preceding parts of this volume, by every impartial reader, that the prayer which bears this title was never intended by him who gave it, to be used as a permanent, precise, verbal form; but that it was designed rather as a general directory for prayer, to point out the things to be prayed for, and the general strain and structure of this exercise, and not the exact words to be employed. If this be so, then the abundant use of this prayer by the Romish Church, and by some Protestant churches, in formally introducing it into every service, and on some occasions three or four times into the service of the same day, seems liable to serious question—as having no adequate warrant, either in the word of God, or in the early usage of the church.

Still the Presbyterian Church regards this prayer with deep veneration, and by no means repudiates the use of it. As dropping from the lips of the Saviour himself, and as marked with so much heavenly wisdom, she regards it with profound respect and esteem, and, like every other part of the inspired word, takes pleasure in manifesting for it unfeigned Christian reverence. She, therefore, both recommends and practises the use of it in her public devotion. Accordingly, our Presbyterian fathers, in the Directory for the Public Worship of God, drawn up and established by the Westminster Assembly of Divines, and afterwards adopted by the General Assembly of the Church of Scotland, speak of the use of this prayer in the following unequivocal and pointed terms. Speaking of 'prayer after sermon,' they say—'And because the prayer which Christ taught his disciples is not only a pattern of prayer, but is itself a most comprehensive prayer, we recommend that it also be used in the prayers of the Church.' This judgment is adopted and expressed, in the same words, by our fathers of the American Church, in the Directory framed by them in 1788.

As Presbyterians, then, we are far from objecting to the repetition of the Lord's Prayer in the public service of the sanctuary. The only question that we ask, is, what shall be the rule for its use? Shall we repeat it always—more than any other words or prayer that were ever uttered by our blessed Lord? Shall we repeat it more than once in the same service, as if there were some magic in its terms? Shall we insist on its repetition, even on occasions on which its language does not appear peculiarly appropriate? We think not. As we are persuaded that it was never intended by our blessed Saviour to be so invariably and formally used; as we do not find a trace of evidence that the apostolic church ever used it thus, or even at all after its establishment in the New Testament form, we cannot suppose the constant use of it to be binding. Yet we believe and teach that the occasional, the frequent use of it, is proper, and sufficient to meet every demand that the most scrupulous regard to the principle of Christian obligation can lay upon us.

I once knew an excellent and popular Presbyterian minister who found it convenient to be systematic in everything. And he was so in regard to the subject under consideration. He closed the last prayer in the morning of every Lord's day with the repetition of the Lord's Prayer; and the whole service every afternoon with the Christian doxology. This is rather too rigidly systematic and formal for me. I have never felt bound or inclined to tie myself to the practice with even so great frequency as this; but have contented myself with using that form, at the close of one of the prayers, once in two, three, or four weeks, so as on the one hand, to testify, that I venerated and loved to use it, and, on the other, that it had not, in my view, any special binding obligation as a form, or any special efficacy as a means.

XIV. It is important to add, that the whole manner of uttering a public prayer should be *in accordance with the humble, filial, affectionate, yet reverential spirit, which ought to characterize the prayer itself throughout*. To hear a prayer uttered in a manner ill in keeping with the sentiments implied, and the petitions expressed; to hear a penitent believing sinner, bowing before the mercy seat, and imploring pardoning mercy and sanctifying grace; confessing total unworthiness of the least favour, while imploring the greatest of all favours, temporal and eternal;—and yet making his appeal to the great Searcher of hearts in a pompous dictatorial manner, is indeed revolting to an enlightened, pious taste. Surely here, if ever, the manner of the suppliant ought to correspond with the humble, contrite spirit which he professes to cherish, and which his words express. The eyes ought to be gently closed, shutting out every scene adapted to arrest the attention, or to break in on that entire abstraction from earth and its affairs which the exercise presupposes. We are expressly told that this was the manner of the preachers in the primitive church. Several of the early fathers tell us that the officiating ministers, in the second and third centuries, always prayed in public 'closing the eyes of the body, and lifting up those of the mind to heaven.' I have known a few ministers of our church who always prayed in public with their eyes wide open, and in some cases evidently looking about the assembly. This was always considered as unfriendly to a devotional spirit, and was connected with disagreeable impressions on the part of the great mass of the worshippers.

The voice ought also to be regulated in a manner adapted to the solemn exercise in which it is employed. The vocal utterance, the tones, and the whole manner of a suppliant who is deeply penitent, and truly in earnest, as they find a response in every human bosom, so they never fail to disclose themselves, and to become manifest whenever they really exist; and, on the other hand, those modulations of the voice in prayer which indicate either the absence of true feeling, or the presence of a dictatorial, haughty, disrespectful spirit toward the greatest and best of beings, never fail to revolt the minds of those who watch the language, and are capable of entering into the spirit of this holy exercise.

In a good public prayer, then, the voice, and the whole manner are made the objects of serious and diligent attention. And as a happy result here cannot be reached by 'mimic attempts,' we can only hope to succeed by having the heart right. If, therefore, we expect our voice, when we lead in this responsible exercise, to convey by every vibration of articulate sound to the ear of every fellow worshipper the idea of humility, contrition of spirit, earnest desire, filial submission, and tender, persevering importunity, we must try, by the grace of God, really to attain this state of mind—really to feel what we utter. We must try to acquire this truly devout, penitent, submissive, and fervent importunity which is so desirable, or we shall never be likely to convey, by sympathy, to the minds of others, the feeling that we are really in earnest.

It may not be improper to subjoin, that the humble, submissive, penitent, pleading modulation of the voice here recommended, ought to be deemed specially appropriate—peculiarly indispensable when we are imploring mercy for a suffering community; pleading for the sick and dying; bewailing the hidings of our Father's face; mourning over the low state of religion; or soliciting the return of his reviving and life-giving Spirit. Here any other posture than the dust of abasement; any other tones than those of the humblest importunity, can hardly be supposed to be tolerated by a believing worshipper.

XV. I have only to add a few remarks in reference to that emphatic word, *Amen!* with which all prayers are commonly ended. This is a word, as is well known, of Hebrew origin, and used, in nearly the same form, in all the dialects of the eastern cognate languages. The original idea which it conveys is that of truth, certainty. Sometimes it is used as a noun; as when Christ (Rev. 1:5) is called the 'Amen, the faithful and true witness.' Sometimes as an adjective; as when we are told (2 Cor. 1:20), that 'all the promises of God are yea and Amen,' i.e., firm, certain, infallible. Sometimes as an adverb, as when our blessed Saviour (John 3:3) said to Nicodemus, '*Verily, verily*, I say unto you, except a man be born again,' etc., that is, truly, truly, or certainly as you live. And sometimes as an interjection, as when the meaning obviously is—Be it so! Let it be as we have said! God grant it!

It would seem, from 1 Corinthians 14:16, that it was customary in the apostolic church for those who united in prayer, to signify their assent to what had been uttered, by saying Amen, at the close. And if this were done wisely, soberly, and with a truly devout spirit, it might still be useful. In the second century, as we are informed by Justin Martyr, at the close of prayer, the people were wont to express their concurrence by saying Amen. And, in the fourth century, Jerome tells us that this practice was carried so far, and accompanied with so much license of voice, in the city of Rome, that the utterance of Amen at the close of prayer was like an outburst of thunder. It is not improbable that some such inconvenient abuse ultimately led to the curbing, if not to the suppression of this popular vociferation.

In the prayers of some churches, the Amen is seldom or never uttered by the officiating minister himself; but always in the form of a response, either by a conspicuous individual, who acts as clerk, or by the mass of the worshippers, or both. In all the Presbyterian churches throughout the world, the officiating minister, it is believed, is in the habit of pronouncing this word himself, which all his fellow worshippers are expected silently to adopt and make their own. And this would seem to be in accordance with the best authorities. Where this word occurs in the book of Psalms, it is evidently added by the same hand that penned the inspired song or prayer, and is not left to be breathed or added by him who reads. In the directory for prayer which our blessed Lord gave to his disciples, he adds the Amen himself, precisely in the manner customary among us. He did not leave it to be supplied by him who heard or adopted the prayer. In all the doxologies with which the inspired apostles close their epistles, the Amen is added by the inspired writer, and not left to be added by one who makes a response. And why should not the man who leads in prayer pronounce this emphatic word himself? Nay, why should he not be expected *a fortiori* to do it; to take the lead in doing it, and by his emphatic example to excite others to more cordiality and more fervour of assent?

But I have much fault to find with the manner in which the Amen is pronounced by many of those who conduct the public devotions of our church. Many pronounce it in that short, rapid manner which divests it at once of all emphasis and all meaning; many in that feeble, inaudible, half-smothered manner which gives it the aspect of anything but the expression of an ardent wish. A few with that protracted 'nasal twang' which confers upon it the character of consummate formality. Only now and then is one heard to pronounce it in that distinct, tender, emphatic manner which indicates real feeling and earnest desire; and which seems to express anything like what the term really imports.

In the word Amen, both syllables ought to be accented. The celebrated orthoepist, Walker, tells us that this is the only word in the English language of two syllables, that has two consecutive accents. If this be so, then the first syllable or letter should be pronounced as *a* in amiable, and be marked with a strong accent; and the second with equal distinctness of accent, as in the syllable formed by the plural of *man*; thus making a clear, distinct, and strongly marked utterance of A-men. This, accompanied with a proper stress of voice, solemnity of manner, and pathos of tone, would make of the devout interjection before us, in effect, and on the popular ear and mind, something like what it was intended to be.

CHAPTER 6

THE BEST MEANS OF ATTAINING EXCELLENCE
IN CONDUCTING PUBLIC PRAYER

EXCELLENCE in this, as well as in the other parts of the public service, is comparative. As in preaching there are rare attainments in eloquence, which few can hope to reach, and which we cannot promise shall be reached by all, however zealously and faithfully they may apply themselves to the study; so in public prayer, a few have risen to a point of happy excellence seldom attained; an excellence flowing from a combination of natural and spiritual accomplishments which can only be expected now and then to meet and shine forth. But, as in preaching, so in prayer, the subject is a proper object of study, and may be expected, in all ordinary cases, to reward, as well as to encourage, faithful and persevering study.

It will not, I trust, be imagined by any that I am about to prescribe a course of preparation for this exercise of a formal, and above all, of a mechanical nature, which, by a sort of human machinery, will insure success. By no means. Nothing is further from my view. But that there *is* an appropriate preparation for it, and a course which may lead to great improvement in it, I cannot doubt; and a preparation corresponding with the spiritual and elevated character of the exercise itself.

The opinion of the venerated fathers of our church on this subject will appear from the following counsel, contained in the fifth chapter of the 'Directory for the Worship of God.' That chapter, entitled 'Of Public Prayer,' after a variety of appropriate directions, thus concludes:

'It is easy to perceive, that in all the preceding directions, there is a very great compass and variety; and it is committed to the judgment and fidelity of the officiating pastor to insist chiefly on such parts, or to take in more or less of the several parts, as he shall be led to, by the aspect of providence; the particular state of the congregation in which he officiates; or the disposition and exercise of his own heart at the time. But we think it necessary to observe, that, although we do not approve, as is well known, of confining ministers to set or fixed forms of prayer for public worship; yet it is the indispensable duty of every minister, previously to his entering on his office, to prepare and qualify himself for this part of his duty, as well as for preaching. He ought, by a thorough acquaintance with the Holy Scriptures; by reading the best writers on the subject; by meditation; and by a life of holy communion with God in secret, to endeavour to acquire both the spirit and the gift of prayer. Not only so; but, when he is to enter on particular acts of worship, he should endeavour to compose his spirit, and to digest his thoughts for prayer, that it may be performed with dignity and propriety, as well as to the profit of those who join in it; and that he may not disgrace that important service by mean, irregular, or extravagant effusions.'

What our venerated fathers place in a later clause in their list of counsels, I wish to stand in the forefront of my suggestions in regard to this subject. I say, therefore, with great confidence,

I. That none can hope to attain excellence in the grace and gift of prayer in the public assembly, *unless they abound in closet devotion, and in holy communion with God in secret.* It is true that, without this, there may be much formal accuracy; much copiousness and variety, both as to topics and language; much rhetorical beauty; much that is unexceptionable both in matter and manner. But, without this, there will not, there cannot be that feeling sense of divine things; that spirit of humble, filial importunity; that holy familiarity with the throne of grace, and with the covenant God who sits upon it, which bespeak one at home in prayer, and whose whole heart is in the exercise. To expect the latter without the former, would be to look for an effect without its necessary cause; would be to expect to see our deficiencies supplied by a constant course of miracles.

The inspired wise man tells us, that 'the heart of the wise teacheth his mouth, and addeth learning to his lips.'[1] Never were these words more remarkably exemplified than in regard to the subject now before us.

It is an old maxim, that no one was ever truly eloquent who did not really and deeply *feel*; who did not truly and heartily enter into the spirit of the subject concerning which he undertook to speak. The maxim is incontrovertibly just; but it is peculiarly and pre-eminently just in regard to public prayer. When the heart is engaged, and in proportion as it

[1] Prov. 16:23.

is deeply and warmly engaged; when the value of spiritual blessings is cordially felt, and the attainment of them earnestly desired; when the soul has a heartfelt sense of its own unworthiness, and an humble, tender confidence in the Saviour's love and grace—in a word, when the whole soul is prepared to flow out in accordance with the language uttered, in faith, love, gratitude and heavenly desire;—then, and only then, will every petition, and word, and tone be, in some good degree, in happy keeping with the nature and scope of the exercise. When the spirit of him who leads the assembly is in this appropriate and happy frame, we may safely trust him in regard to all that shall flow from his lips.

It cannot be doubted that a defect here is one of the most abundant sources of faults in public prayer. Hence the frigid, unfeeling accuracy, so often observable in this part of the service of the sanctuary. Hence the hesitation, the embarrassment, and the various improprieties so frequently witnessed in the public prayers of able and pious men. They have not come from their knees in private to the services of the sacred desk. They have not come with hearts reeking with the hallowed influences of the closet, to be the leaders of the Lord's host in the sanctuary. The consequence is, their hearts are cold. Though, perhaps, not strangers to the grace of God, they have not so often, or so recently as they ought to have done, summoned them, as it were, into the divine presence, and so laboured to impress them with a sense of their own poverty and weakness, and of the divine glory, as to make every confession and petition the unfeigned utterance of the heart. How much more will all these defects be likely to be, not only really, but sensibly aggravated, if there be not only a state of present coldness, but, as we have too much reason to fear there may sometimes be, the entire absence of experimental piety!

Many years ago, when I was a pastor in a neighbouring city, a beloved and eminently pious brother occupied, by invitation, my pulpit; and rich indeed were the services which he performed. His sermon was pious, instructive, and excellent; but his prayers were peculiarly appropriate, rich, and impressive; indeed in what might not improperly be called a superior style of importunate, touching devotion. I was struck with this when engaged in uniting with my excellent brother; but still more, when, on withdrawing from the sanctuary, an aged mother in Israel said to me in passing, 'That man prays as if he lived at the throne of grace.'

And hence it is, no doubt, that we sometimes meet with men of comparatively weak minds, of very small attainments in human knowledge, and in every respect unqualified advantageously to address an assembly in continued discourse, who were yet peculiarly excellent and edifying in social prayer. There they appeared in their element; happy in thought; ready and striking in expression; and uttering themselves with all that unembarrassed, simple, filial, touching manner which flowed from a mind perfectly familiar with the throne of grace, and daily accustomed to spread their wants and desires before it on all manner of subjects. We have seen such deeply spiritual men, when suddenly called upon to officiate on an unusual occasion, without the least hesitation, engaging in the service, and going through it with all the childlike ease, fluency, and enlargement which indicated that they were accustomed to plead with the Hearer of prayer in secret, on all manner of subjects relating to Christian experience, and to the state of the church and the world. I have been sometimes surprised and delighted to find plain unlettered men performing this duty with a readiness and richness both of thought and expression, superior to those exhibited by many learned and eloquent divines; convincing every fellow worshipper that they had acquired the precious gift not by literary study or discipline, but by habitual and intimate communion with God, and the daily practice of pleading with him for the riches of his grace, and embodying in simple, familiar language all the desires of their hearts.

We are told of the great Reformer, Martin Luther, that his public prayers had a life, a power, a heartiness, a wrestling importunity of the most remarkable kind. But we are told of the same wonderful man that he spent from three to four hours every day in his closet, pleading with God for blessings on his own soul and ministry, and on the great cause in which he was engaged.

If, then, any desire to make happy attainments, and progressive improvement both in the grace and the gift of public prayer, the closet will be found the appropriate and the most important nursery. If the object be to train the heart to believing and delightful intercourse with heaven, and the lips to a simple, affectionate, and happy utterance of the desires of the heart, where can we find a place or an employment so directly and happily adapted to gain our purpose, as the altar of private devotion, to which we resort for holding communion with God in secret; where, upon our bended knees, we read and study the word of God, and strive to transplant its diction and its spirit into our own souls? Surely this is the place, and this the employment in which the soul is to be nurtured to spiritual views, to holy desires, to faith, and love, and joy. This is the place and this the employment in which, by the aid of the Holy Spirit, we may expect to make progress in holy intimacy with God, and in that sanctified and feeling fervour which is the parent of all genuine importunity in prayer. In a word, this is the place, and this the employment in which, under God, the spiritual taste is to be purified, the spiritual appetite increased, the affections lifted up to heaven, and the lips touched as with a live coal from off God's holy altar to speak his praise.

We may safely say, then, that no man ever attained any high degree of excellence in public prayer, who had not previously cultivated peculiar intimacy with his covenant God in secret devotion; who did not abound in closet prayer; who had not had his heart trained to more than common familiarity with, and affection for, new covenant blessings; and his tongue loosened to pour out spiritual desires without reserve or faltering. I would certainly place this in the front rank of all means to be employed for the attainment in question. He that would be acceptable and powerful in public prayer, must know something habitually of what is meant by 'wrestling with God' in his closet: must be 'mighty' in secret prayer, as well as in the Scriptures. He who neglects this, or who has little taste for this, might as well expect a miracle to be wrought for his help every time he enters the pulpit. The kind of excellence in this service which we wish to see, 'goeth not out but by prayer and fasting.'

II. Another means, not so essential, and yet highly important, if any desire to attain excellence in public prayer, is, not only to *read*, but to *study* some of the best books which have treated of this subject.

If anyone in giving counsel to a candidate for the holy ministry, to prepare him for preaching, should omit to refer him to the best authors who have treated of sermonizing, he would be regarded as a most defective counsellor. And the candidate who, after such authors had been recommended to him, should undervalue and neglect them, would be deemed altogether demented.—Surely it is no less unwise to disregard similar aid in reference to that part of the public service which is now under consideration. Though many ministers of the gospel appear to be altogether unconscious of the value of this help, or of their personal need of it, yet some eminently pious and learned divines have made a very different estimate, and have employed themselves in giving detailed counsel on this subject, and in making large collections of scriptural texts for the aid of the young and inexperienced. My impression is, that, however such books may be disregarded by the superficial and the ignorant, the wiser and the better furnished of the sacred order have ever regarded them with favour, and made the highest estimate of their value.

Among the most respectable of these writers are, Bishop [John] Wilkins, [1614–72], of the Church of England, who, though a prelate of that church, was a warm advocate for the privilege of extemporary or free prayer;[1] the Rev. Matthew Henry [1662–1714], the far-famed commentator

[1] A Discourse concerning the Gift of Prayer, showing what it is, wherein it consists, and how far it is attainable by industry—8vo. 1670.

on the Bible;[1] the Rev. Nathaniel Vincent [*c*. 1639–97], a pious and learned divine of London, in the seventeenth century;[2] and the Rev. Dr Watts [1674–1748], whose praise is in all the churches of Christ.[3] The object of all these excellent writers was, not merely to illustrate and urge the nature and importance of prayer in general, but to furnish aid, especially to the young and inexperienced, who desire to make improvement both in the grace and the gift of extemporary, social, and public prayer. To these may be added the numerous writers who have published large collections of forms of prayer, for the closet, the family, and the prayer-meeting. Of these, Jenks, Bishop Andrews, Bishop Kenn, Bennet, Jeremy Taylor, Scott, and Jay, are among the best.[4] Not that they are all equally clear

---

[1] *A Method for Prayer, with Scripture expressions proper to be used under each head*—8vo. 1710. [A new edition of this valuable work, prepared by Dr O. Palmer Robertson, was published by the Trust in 2010 under the title *A Way to Pray*.]

[2] *The Spirit of Prayer, wherein the nature of prayer is opened, the kinds of prayer are handled, and the right manner of praying discovered*, etc.— 12mo. 1677.

[3] *A Guide to Prayer*, etc.—12mo. 1730 [reprinted by the Trust in 2001.

[4] [Benjamin Jenks (1646–1724) Rector of Harley, in Shropshire. *Prayers and Offices of Devotion for Families, and for Particular Persons, upon Most Occasions* (London, 1697). Lancelot Andrewes (1555–1626), Bishop of Winchester. *The private devotions of the Right Reverend Father in God Lancelot Andrewes* (London, 1647). Thomas Kenn (or Ken, 1637–1711). *A Manual of Prayer* (Winchester *c*. 1665). Benjamin Bennet (*c*. 1674–1726). *The Christian Oratory, or the Devotion of the Closet Displayed* (London, 1725). Jeremy Taylor (1613–67) *The golden grove, or, A manuall of daily prayers and letanies, fitted to the dayes of the week containing a short summary of what is to be believed, practised, desired*, etc. (London, 1655). John Scott (1639–95). *The Christian Life from its beginning to its Consummation in Glory ... with directions for*

and sound in their evangelical views; but they are all rich
in devotional topics and language, and furnish, to the
enlightened and thinking student, those materials out of
which, if he be not greatly in fault, he may add largely to his
devotional stores. We, not infrequently, derive some of our
best thoughts and happiest expressions from conversation
with those from whom we differ most entirely both in spirit
and opinion. The most truly valuable use we can make of
any book, especially one on such a subject, is by no means
servilely copying its pages; but by digesting its thoughts;
by making them our own; and, in short, like a spiritual
chemist, subjecting its matter to those various analyses and
modifications which both the imagination and the heart can
often apply to the most perverse and intractable materials.

It is, perhaps, not unjust to say, that the prevailing
mistake of young preachers is to undervalue and neglect
such elementary works as I have described, partly from
unconsciousness of their own defects, and partly from the
notion that such works are rather beneath them. It is storied
of the late Principal Robertson, the celebrated historian,
and for many years the venerated leader of the moderate
party in the Church of Scotland, that he was often solicited
by candidates for the ministry in that church, to give them
instruction and counsel with respect to their studies,
especially in the earlier stages of them. Though he was far
from being himself evangelical in the general character
of his mind and preaching; yet we are told that he never

---

private devotion and forms of prayer fitted to the several states of Chris-
tians (London, 1681). William Jay (*The Domestic Minister's Assistant; Or,*
Prayers for the Use of Families (2nd ed. Bath, 1820).]

failed to advise such inquirers to begin by studying with great care Vincent on the 'Shorter Catechism.'[1] And when they gave a response, as they often did, which satisfied him that they considered Vincent's work as beneath them, that is, too simple and elementary to be studied by those who had risen above the classes of catechized children, he often replied—'Young man, you mistake the matter. That book, though simple and elementary in its character, is full of sound theology, and of methodized mature thought. If you master that work, and impress it thoroughly on your mind, you will have accomplished far more than you imagine. You will have laid the foundation for safe, systematic thinking, and for that course of didactic instruction which it will be the business of your life to pursue.' This counsel was worthy of the sagacity of that Presbyterian rationalist. He knew that these young men were expected to preach in conformity with the Confession of Faith and other formularies of the Church of Scotland; and he was perfectly aware that they could take no step better adapted to prepare them for performing that work in the most acceptable and useful manner, than to begin by making themselves masters of a work which, though adapted to instruct and benefit the most untutored youth who had the least intelligence, was fitted also to enlighten and feed the most mature and vigorous mind.

It is a good sign, therefore, when candidates for the holy ministry do not feel too wise to be taught; when they do

[1] Thomas Vincent, an elder brother of Nathaniel , mentioned in a preceding paragraph, who wrote on Prayer. [Reprinted by the Trust in the Puritan Paperback series as *The Shorter Catechism Explained from Scripture* (1980, 2021).

not 'despise the day of small things'; when they are willing to read and to impress upon their memories sound, clear, elementary treatises on every department of the public service. Such a spirit affords a pledge that they are willing to listen to the dictates of wisdom and experience, and will be apt to lay a foundation for those mature and solid attainments which cannot fail to last long, and to wear well.

Let a candidate for the holy ministry, then, take *all* the books which have been mentioned, if they be all within his reach: let him read them carefully, taking pains to impress their leading contents on his memory: let him make such written notes on the several parts as may serve at once to aid his memory, and impart order and system to his views: and, finally, having done this with great care, not only during the term of his preliminary studies, but also often during the first ten years of his ministerial labours: let him not disdain the occasional use of them for the same purpose, as long as he lives: remembering that in this, as well as with regard to many other things, every minister of the gospel ought to be a close student, and a diligent learner to the end of life. One of the evils against which every minister who values either his Master's honour, or his own usefulness, ought sacredly and constantly to guard, not once only, but to his last breath, is the tendency in aged ministers to grow careless, or, at least, greatly to relax their attention to this matter. The infirmities of the aged unavoidably bring with them so many things which make large demands on the indulgence of those around them, that a wise man, when he approaches the closing scene of life, will strive to let these infirmities be as few, and as little prominent as he possibly can.

III. Another means of attaining excellence in public prayer, is *to store the mind with the language and the riches of the word of God.*

It was mentioned, in a preceding chapter, as an important element of excellence in a good public prayer, that it should abound in the language of Scripture. If this be the case, then the best means of enriching our prayers with this precious element, must be considered as worthy of serious attention and inquiry. In this inquiry, it is the object of the present section to afford aid.

If we examine the word of God with a discriminating eye, and with a mind ready to absorb, and appropriate to the devout element, whatever can be legitimately so appropriated, we shall find that every book and every chapter, from Genesis to the Apocalypse, affords ample stores for our purpose. In all the historical books, we shall find facts stated, principles expressed or implied, or allusions conveyed, which, without any conceit or unnatural forcing, admit of the happiest application and use in prayer. Thus the process of creation; the command to the light to shine out of darkness; the entrance of sin into the world; the expulsion from paradise; the sacrifices of Cain and Abel, with their different results; the overwhelming flood which sin brought upon the world of the ungodly; the call of Abraham; the going down into Egypt; the bondage of the people there; their deliverance by the hand of Moses; the passage of the destroying angel over the land of Egypt; the deliverance of the Israelites by the sprinkling of blood on the door posts of their dwellings; the departure of their armies; the pursuit of Pharaoh; the destruction of his host in the Red Sea; the subsistence of the congregation on manna in the wilderness; their many murmurings and rebellions there; their entrance into Canaan; their protracted wars in expelling the Canaanites; etc., etc., may all be rendered subservient to the devotions of the sanctuary; not to be lugged in, in a clumsy, didactic, and simply historical style; but either by such remote allusion, or such direct reference as may at once gratify the most literary and the most devout taste.

To illustrate my meaning, if there were occasion in prayer to plead the cause of a whole church, or any particular part of it, encompassed and struggling with difficulty, what could be more adapted to touch the feelings, and warm the hearts of devout worshippers, than to plead in some such way as the following: 'O thou who didst of old, deliver thy covenant people from the bondage of Egypt, and didst open a way through the sea for them to pass in safety; so may it please thee now to deliver thy afflicted and struggling church, to disappoint those who seek her hurt, to sanctify to her all her troubles, and bring her out of them all with increasing purity, and peace, and joy.' Or, supposing we had occasion to bewail the slavery of sin, and to pray for deliverance from the bondage of corruption, we might say—'We are by nature carnal, sold under sin; but we rejoice to know that, as thou didst once bring thy people out of bondage, and make them the Lord's freemen in their own land; so thou hast promised, by the Lord Jesus Christ, to proclaim liberty to the captives, and the opening of the prison to them that are the bond slaves of Satan. We rejoice to read in thy word, that, as Moses lifted up the serpent in the wilderness, even so the Son of Man has been lifted up, that whosoever believeth on him should not perish, but obtain eternal life.' And again: 'We bless thee that when the destroying angel received his commission to go forth, and to smite the firstborn with disease and death, thou didst, by the sprinkling of blood, give thy people a pledge of life; so we pray that now, amidst the multitudes who are dying around us, many may be sprinkled by that blood which cleanseth from all sin, and which alone can prepare for the abodes of peace and love.' Or again: 'We thank thee that, when thou wast about to bring a flood upon the world of the ungodly, thou didst provide an ark for saving one man, righteous in his generation, and his family; so now we praise thee that thou hast provided a greater and better ark for saving all of our world of sinners who are willing to enter in. O that multitudes in the midst of us might be made willing in a day of thy power!'

Now, as the recollection of these historical references can be expected to occur readily and seasonably only to those who remember and study them; and as the appositeness of their occurrence, and the felicity of their application will depend not a little on the degree in which the minds of individuals are habituated to run in that channel; it follows that every minister of the gospel who desires to prepare himself in the best manner for this part of the public service, ought to read every part of the word of God with a view to this application of it; pondering in his mind the use that might be made of every record, and thus making every portion of his scriptural reading subservient to his public work. It is my fixed opinion, that if ministers and candidates for the ministry were in the habit of reading the Bible with as fixed and strong a purpose, and as earnest an endeavour to make it all subservient to their improvement in public prayer, as in public preaching, we should find new richness and glory shed on the devotional exercises of the sanctuary.

But it would be wise to go further than has been suggested. I would earnestly recommend that portions of the word of God be every day, and certainly every week, carefully committed to memory, with a particular view to their use in public prayer. While every part of the word of God, as we have already seen, may be made an auxiliary in appropriate and happy prayer, it is well known that there are other parts which furnish large and precious examples of prayer itself, or of that which easily admits of being thrown into the form of most tender, importunate, and elevated prayer. The whole book of Psalms furnishes an example of what we here mean. We may consider this portion of the word of God the great storehouse of devotional composition, many parts of which every minister ought to have carefully deposited in his memory, and to be able, at will, to produce them in the sacred desk. In like manner, the writings of all the prophets, and especially those of Isaiah and Daniel, present much matter which will strike every judicious minister as exceedingly rich in materials for public devotion. And with these every part of the New Testament teems, more particularly the apostolical epistles, and the Revelation of John the Divine. Let large portions of these be faithfully committed to memory, and the recollection of them with ease be insured by a frequent repetition of the deposit. It was said of the late celebrated John Brown, of Haddington, probably one of the most truly and deeply devout men that Scotland ever contained, that he had the whole Bible committed to memory so far as that if any verse in the whole volume were mentioned in his presence, he could instantly tell where it was to be found, and repeat the preceding and following verses. Surely this is an attainment unspeakably desirable for a minister of the gospel, and which it is easy to see might be made to bear in the happiest manner not only on his preaching, but also on every form of excellence in public prayer.

It is to be presumed, of course, that every minister of the gospel reads a portion of the Bible with a view to his own spiritual edification, every day that he lives; and that he does this at greater length on the Lord's day than on other days, and on that day with peculiar application of mind. Now if every minister, in reading the word of God, at any time, but especially on the morning of the Lord's day, were to do it with the express purpose of furnishing his memory and his heart with some portion of materials for the public prayers of that day, could he fail of being aided by it in that part of his public labours? It has been already suggested that *variety*, under proper regulation, is an important quality in the devotions of the sanctuary. Could a more direct and efficient course be taken to secure a desirable portion of this element in its best form than to labour, every successive Sabbath, to derive from the great fountain of all revealed truth, something 'new as well as old,' for the services of the following day? Perhaps among all the methods devised of guarding against that wearisome *sameness* which is so apt to be perceptible in the public prayers of those who very often, and for a long course of years, officiate in this exercise, that which I have last mentioned, would, if faithfully and perseveringly followed, prove most effectual. Would not even the aged and the infirm, in the decline of life, if they spent an hour, or even half that time, every Sabbath morning, in laying up something for the public devotions of that day, much more frequently than they do, escape that appearance of carelessness and want of interest in public prayer which is so apt to creep into the public prayers of aged and infirm ministers?

It was originally my intention to include in this manual an extended collection of passages from the word of God for the purpose of furnishing materials on all subjects for the devotions of the pulpit. But I have been deterred from carrying into execution this part of my original plan by three reasons. First, such a collection, to be of real value, must be large; which would have swelled the size and expense of the volume to an inconvenient degree. Secondly, Bishop Wilkins, Mr Henry, Dr Watts, and others, have already made a collection of this kind quite as large and complete as I could have thought of. Of course, the work is already done, and need not be repeated. Thirdly, if a young minister wishes to derive the greatest benefit from such a collection, it will do him most good to make it for himself. In studying a classical author in an unknown language, a literal translation put into the hands of the student is always an injury rather than a help. If he is left to find out the knowledge of every sentence by his own labour, his knowledge will be better digested, and will dwell more firmly in his memory. So, if the youthful candidate for the pulpit should search the Scriptures for himself, and make the collection recommended, from time to time, by his personal labour, it would be more thoroughly his own, and be more likely to be always at hand to serve his purpose.

IV. Another method of attaining excellence in public prayer, is, when any dispensation of providence occurs, which appears to demand special attention in the devotions of the sanctuary, to make *prompt* and *special preparation* for presenting that object in public prayer in the most simple, scriptural, and edifying form. He who occupies the place of a public teacher and guide, whose duty it is to enlighten the public mind, and to give an impulse to public feeling, ought to be constantly on the watch that he may be enabled to perform his duty in a skilful and happy manner; and when anything unusual occurs it ought, of course, to be matter of immediate and solicitous inquiry with him how he may give a touch to the ark of God, in relation to the matter in question, which will be likely to issue in the greatest amount of good to the souls committed to his charge.

It was my privilege, in early life, to be somewhat acquainted with a venerable minister of Massachusetts, who went further than any other pastor I can now call to mind in adapting his preaching to all the remarkable dispensations of Providence that occurred. He not only preached in a very appropriate manner on all fast and thanksgiving days, whether appointed by the general or state governments, but he was accustomed to take a public notice in the pulpit of all occurrences which were adapted strongly to occupy and excite the public mind—a protracted and distressing drought; a destructive flood; an extensively injurious fire or storm; a remarkable eclipse; a singularly distressing case of suicide; the opening of a magnificent bridge; a noted case of appeal to witchcraft; all these furnished this good man, from time to time, with themes for pulpit discourses, many of which were afterwards given to the public from the press, and yet remain monuments of his vigilance and fidelity.

This practice was wise. Whatever the event may be which strongly occupies the popular feeling, and excites to much conversation, it is capable of being turned to valuable account by a wise and faithful minister of the gospel. And this consideration extends to public prayer as well as preaching. Nay, a wise pastor will often find occasion to take a seasonable and delicate notice of a recent occurrence in prayer, which he would hesitate to make the subject of a sermon, or formally to introduce into a discourse. Now it is always of some importance, and sometimes of very great importance to the edification of a Christian assembly, that these notices of recent events in the devotional exercises of the pulpit be scriptural, judicious, and such as are adapted to meet the feelings, and gratify the taste of enlightened Christian worshippers.

I have sometimes gone to the house of God when some recent occurrence of deep and thrilling interest filled every heart, and dwelt upon every tongue; and when I expected a feeling impression of it to warm the mind, and shine forth in the prayers of the officiating minister. But, to my disappointment and mortification, I have sometimes found him as totally silent on the subject, as if the intelligence had never reached his ears, and allowing all the excited feelings of those around him to pass away without any of those appeals to the throne of grace which are adapted at once to compose, to soothe, and to elevate the soul of the devout worshipper.

But, at some other times, I have found the officiating minister, on these exciting occasions, not silent, indeed, in regard to them, but praying in a manner in no respect preferable to silence. I have known him to utter himself in prayer in such a hesitating, embarrassed, injudicious manner, as plainly evinced that he had not bestowed a thought on the manner in which he should order his petitions. The consequence was, that instead of meeting and consulting the excited feelings of the assembly, he rather gave pain, and banished all sentiments of devotion.

This is unhappy; and every minister who desires to promote the edification of the church ought to be on the watch to guard against such embarrassing circumstances, and to prepare himself, on all such special occasions, to present his petitions in that simple, scriptural, and happy manner which shall be adapted to satisfy every mind, and to warm every heart. This is, no doubt, what our fathers meant, when, in the directions for the performance of public prayer, quoted in the beginning of this chapter, they say—'When he is to enter on particular acts of worship, he should endeavour to compose his spirit, and to digest his thoughts for prayer, that it may be performed with dignity and propriety, as well as to the profit of those who join in it.' In this preparation, the stores of the word of God furnish, of course, the best aid. Scarcely any exigency, joyful or adverse, can occur, in regard to which the inspired pages do not exhibit appropriate forms of petition. If these heavenly stores were studied and treasured up by ministers as they ought to be, they would be at no loss for appropriate language in which to present any object before the throne of grace; and even with regard to the most unusual occurrence, the reflection of a few minutes would supply them with all that they need. How worthy of censure is that minister who, in the midst of occurrences which occupy every heart, and dwell upon every tongue, will not spend a thought in preparing to present before the throne in the most acceptable manner those petitions in which so many around him feel a deep and tender interest!

V. The last means of attaining excellence in public prayer that I shall mention, is, *the habit of devotional composition.*

It is perfectly known, to every well-informed person, that we, as Presbyterians, are entirely and irreconcilably opposed to *confining* ministers to prescribed forms of prayer. It has been demonstrated, if I mistake not, in a preceding chapter, that such a practice was wholly unknown in the primitive and apostolic church; that it was never introduced until about five hundred years after the death of Christ, when Christian knowledge and piety had greatly declined; and when many corruptions, over which intelligent Christians mourned, had crept into the church; and that its introduction and establishment have been connected with a number of most serious evils.

Still we do not pronounce all use of precomposed prayers to be criminal, and have no doubt that devotional composition may be so employed as to minister most happily to the attainment of the best attributes of public prayer.

I would by no means, indeed, recommend to anyone, in any case, to write prayers; to commit them to memory;

and to recite them *verbatim* in the pulpit. I have never been personally acquainted with anyone who did this; though I have heard of it in a very few instances, but always in a way, and under impressions that satisfied me it was not an eligible method, but adapted rather to generate formality, and could not fail of proving unfriendly to the most enlightened and successful culture of the gift of prayer; that precious gift, which ought to be highly prized, and diligently cherished by every gospel minister, and which enters more deeply into the acceptance and usefulness of the sacred office than any statement of mine can represent.

It is not to be supposed that there is anything about extempore prayer, more than about the other services of the pulpit, which will enable anyone who attempts it, to do well without mental discipline; without mature knowledge; without a happy command of language; without some taste and skill in the selection of topics; and some facility, the result of habit, as well as of grace, in the choice of simple, plain, yet appropriate diction. And these things must not be expected to come by inspiration. Means must, of course, be employed to attain them. Lord Chancellor Bacon has somewhere said—'Reading makes a *full* man; conversation a *ready* man, and writing an *exact* man.' This maxim is not only just, but it is applicable to every department of knowledge and of mental exercise. He who wishes to discipline his own mind on any subject; to render his habits of thinking accurate and profound; to cure himself of habits of crude thought, and loose expression, ought to make a point of subjecting every matter that he takes in hand to the process of writing; and he will be more likely to attain his object than by any other human means in his power. If a man wished to study a subject with most entire success; to attain deep, clear, and systematic views of it in all its parts, he could not take a better course than to write a treatise upon it. However confident he might be, before he took his pen in hand, that he understood the subject well; he would soon find that the precision of thought and of language which he felt imposed upon him, compelled him to extend his information, to rectify his conceptions, and to modify his definitions at every step.

These are precisely the correctives which writing affords in the case of those who are immature and unfurnished for the able and happy performance of extemporaneous public prayer. The most common faults of such in this exercise, are poverty of appropriate, comprehensive, seasonable thought, and the want of a judicious, happy style of expression. Now, next to a warm and feeling heart, there can be no surer corrective of these faults than careful, devout writing. Nay, many a man of warm and feeling heart has given vent to pious effusions in prayer, which he could never have uttered if they had undergone that careful inspection, and calm review which the process of committing to paper necessarily furnishes. Though fervour of piety is the most important of all elements as a preparation for public prayer; yet even this will not secure a man against all the faults incident to this exercise; nay, his very fervour may betray him into modes of expression, which cannot stand the test of enlightened and sanctified reflection, and of which he would in no way be so likely to perceive the real character as by subjecting them to the inspection and discipline of the eye as well as of the feelings.

If, therefore, we desire to have our words, in all our solemn approaches to the throne of grace, according to the divine prescription, 'few and well ordered'; if we desire to have our petitions 'well considered,' and our language such as is best adapted to impress and to edify the people of God, can we doubt that it is wise to ponder well what we utter before the Lord, and to subject it to that solemn and leisurely review of which the process of writing gives so ample an opportunity? The object of writing in this case, is not to be refined; not to be rhetorical; not to be elegant or beautiful; not to aim at elaborate ingenuity; but, precisely the reverse;—to study brevity, simplicity, comprehensiveness, and adaptedness to every capacity; to study that which is natural, plain, perfectly intelligible to the humblest worshipper; and adapted to meet the feelings at once of the highest and lowest of the assembly. I know not how this is to be attained in the happiest and best manner but by the habit of devotional composition; by a happy selection and adjustment of topics; by weighing language; and by employing all the means in our power to make the most scriptural matter, and the most scriptural manner of addressing the throne of grace, familiar to our minds.

The late Dr Witherspoon, whose counsels to theological students have always been highly prized, was accustomed to embrace the following anecdote in the course of his lectures to this class of his pupils. The Rev. Dr John Gillies, one of the ministers of Glasgow, was one of the most pious, warm-hearted, popular divines of the Church of Scotland in his day. He was greatly distinguished as a friend of revivals of religion, and as taking a lively interest in everything connected with the success of the gospel. His 'Historical Collections,' in two volumes 8vo., published in 1754, giving an account of remarkable revivals of religion, both in Europe and America, bear ample testimony to this aspect of his character.[1]

Dr Witherspoon remarked, that the public prayers of this gentleman were, on the whole, the best he ever heard. They were not what many would call beautiful or eloquent. But in simplicity; in richness of appropriate thought; in spirituality; in the constant recognition of the richest evangelical sentiments; in pathos; in variety; in perfect appropriateness to every occasion on which he officiated; in scriptural language happily selected, and admirably applied; in short, in all the attributes of an humble, filial, touching prayer, adapted to all capacities, but especially acceptable to the most fervently pious of his congregation, he exceeded all men he had ever heard in the sacred desk. Dr Witherspoon observed, that he one day said to Dr Gillies: 'Brother, I have always admired your gift in prayer as remarkable and peculiar. Will you allow me to ask how you attained that power?' Dr Gillies replied as follows: 'My dear brother, I do not allow that there is anything so remarkable in my prayers as you seem disposed to intimate. They do not appear to me to deserve the commendation which your question seems to imply. But if there be anything in my public prayers different from the most common place and ordinary services of that kind, I must ascribe it, under

[1] [A title reprinted by the Trust in 1981.]

God, to the unwearied pains I have taken, for many years, to improve in this branch of my ministerial work. In the early part of my ministry I abounded in devotional composition. Indeed I may say, that for the first ten years of my pastoral life, I never wrote a sermon, without writing a prayer, in part or in whole, corresponding with it in its general strain. This gave me the habit of expressing myself in prayer on all manner of subjects in appropriate, well-considered, and scriptural terms, and enabled me to embrace a variety in my public devotional exercises which I should not have been likely otherwise to reach.'

Whether Dr Gillies was in the habit of committing the prayers which he thus diligently wrote, verbatim to memory, and strictly reciting them in the pulpit, he does not appear to have stated; but if he did, it certainly was not the wisest course, and was one which I would by no means recommend as best adapted to answer the end proposed. The unavoidable effect of such a course would be to restrain the 'gift' of prayer in its best fervours; to confer upon the whole service more of an artificial and studied aspect; to make the exercise an affair of the intellect rather than of the heart; and to generate, in spite of every effort that could be made to avoid it, cold formality rather than that 'fervent and effectual prayer which availeth much' in him who offers, as well as in regard to him to whom it is addressed.

My impression is, that the very process of composing such prayers is the most important part of the benefit which they confer. Were each one to be thrown into the fire as soon as it was completed, the great end of its composition would be in a good measure gained. That end is the continual enlargement of the devotional resources, and the devotional taste of the individual who writes. Every time, therefore, that he takes pen in hand to form an address to the throne of grace, if he conduct it aright, he benefits both his heart and his head;—his heart, by summoning it to contemplate the most exalted and glorious of all objects; to acknowledge the most weighty and solemn of all obligations; and to supplicate the most precious of all favours, temporal and spiritual;—and his head, by selecting and weighing topics; by pondering on the proprieties of devotional language; and by studying how to make his words as 'few and well-ordered,' as simple, as scriptural, and as richly comprehensive as possible.

The fault of many ministers in public prayer is abounding in unnecessary words; and of others that they are prone to employ unsuitable, canting, and unmeaning words. Now I know of no more effectual method of correcting both these classes of faults than the enlightened, careful and deliberate use of the pen. The moment the eye of an educated man rests on an incorrect or untasteful expression committed to paper, he seldom fails to detect at once its inappropriate character.

I have said, that I would by no means advise anyone to be in the habit of committing written prayers to memory, and reciting them servilely in the pulpit. There is something in the practice of uttering anything in public from memory that is apt to beget in the speaker, in spite of every effort to the contrary, a formal reciting tone. This principle seldom fails to be exemplified very strikingly in *memoriter* preachers. In the course of a long life, and with some range of opportunity for observation on this subject, I have never heard more than one, or, at most, two memoriter preachers who entirely, avoided the reciting tone. The same principle applies, in some measure, to prayers recited from memory. I do not believe that it is, ordinarily, possible wholly to divest them of the character and tone of recitation. It is one of the rarest things in the world to hear, anyone read a prayer, or any other composition, in the perfectly simple, natural intonation which is, of course, employed in extemporaneous, feeling, animated utterance. The same difficulty applies to reciting from memory. The formal reading tone will seldom fail to creep in, and disclose to the practised ear that the man is uttering something studied and prepared.

While, therefore, I would earnestly exhort every young minister and candidate for the sacred office to abound in devotional composition, for the sake of enlarging his devotional resources, both as to topics and language, and also as the most effectual means of imparting to his whole style the simplicity, the variety, and the scriptural richness so desirable in that important exercise; I would quite as earnestly advise that the plan of servile recitation from memory be sacredly avoided. The true plan is to write often; to write much; to store the mind with ample furniture for the exercise; but to leave the utterance of the moment to the impulses of a feeling, gushing heart. The occasion must be very peculiar, and the circumstances very delicate indeed, in which I should be willing to recommend repeating, in the public assembly, the *ipsissima verba* which had been written.

I take for granted that every candidate for the ministry, and every minister of the gospel will, every year, observe days of special prayer and humiliation, accompanied at proper seasons, with fasting. Such days will ever be found important in nurturing a spirit of piety, and will not be neglected by him who wishes and studies to grow in grace. Now a wise minister, or candidate for the ministry, will ever make the observance of such days subservient to devotional composition. They will lead him to pen many an address to the great Head of the church in regard to the various objects which occupy, in succession, the most prominent places on these various days. And if he seize with intelligence and with faithfulness the spirit of each occasion, he will be constrained to pour out his feelings on paper, in regard to national calamities, and national mercies; in regard to the state of the church and the world; in regard to the passing events in providence, and the desertions or the triumphs of divine grace; in regard to prevailing sickness, or joyful health; in regard to the changes of the seasons, and the fruits of the earth; and especially in regard to the conflicts and enjoyments of his own soul. Now, when a man is led by these sacred exercises in private to study how he may most happily and acceptably express the devout aspirations of his heart on all these subjects, and is wise enough to be in the habit of putting on paper the exercises of his own mind on all these occasions, they may, and will be made subservient to his ability to conduct the devotions of the sanctuary in the most appropriate, happy, and acceptable manner; with all the variety, simplicity and richness that can be desired.

But while devotional composition ought always to be connected with these days of special observance, and to make a part of that record of such days which may afterwards be seriously and devoutly reviewed; yet it might by no means to be confined to those days. A wise minister, when he finds his heart made specially to feel, or his mind, by any circumstances, drawn into a happy train of thought or expression adapted to public devotion, will seize upon it, and take the first opportunity of committing it to writing, that he may improve his devotional vocabulary, and enlarge his devotional treasures. He who has a taste for divine contemplation, or for converse with heaven; or a mind awake to all the impressions which the conversation of the pious, or the complaints or profaneness of the wicked may sometimes suggest, will be at no loss to understand how they may all be made subservient to the purpose under consideration.

If I shall succeed in convincing the reader of these pages that no man can be expected to attain much excellence in this department of the public service of the sanctuary, who does not feel the importance of this excellence; who is not willing to take pains to attain it; who does not commune much with his God in secret; who does not pray without ceasing for both the grace and the gift of prayer; and who is not constantly on the watch to embrace the opportunities and the means to this end which may be placed within his reach, to gain improvement, my purpose will be in some measure gained. Until these impressions and habits are acquired, there is no hope of much advance in this happy accomplishment. A man may, indeed, upon cheaper terms, learn the art of making an 'eloquent prayer,' nay, a 'splendid prayer'; a prayer that shall send the worldly and the superficial away praising it to the skies; but not that prayer which 'entereth into the ears of the Lord of Sabaoth,' which will meet the wishes of the people of God, and which is adapted to draw down blessings upon the church of God.

We call that preacher wise, who is ever desiring and striving to make improvement in the precious art of reaching and impressing the hearts of men, and 'winning souls to Christ'; who labours to 'bring out of his treasure things new and old'; who is awake to every occurrence, in nature or in grace, which may suggest to him a new topic of impressive address, or a new form of language likely to find access to the hearts of any class of his hearers. We commend the wisdom of that preacher who does not open a book, or take a walk, or engage in a journey, or enter a company, or look abroad on the face of nature, without trying to find something to add to his store of means in preaching Christ to his perishing fellow men. Surely it is an equal mark of wisdom when the occupant of the sacred desk is equally anxious, and equally diligent in striving and praying to derive from all sources the means of improvement in conducting the devotions of the sanctuary. And if so, how shall we estimate either the judgment or the fidelity of him, who spares no pains to improve, enrich, and elevate the character of his *sermons*, from week to week, while that of his *public prayers* seems to engage but little thought; to call forth little or no effort; is marked with little or no improvement; and goes on from year to year, in the same dull routine, as a mere secondary concern? Feeling myself near to my last account, I would put it to the consciences of my younger brethren in the ministry (with the aged, I dare not, for more reasons than one, remonstrate) how they can reconcile it with their views of duty, thus to undervalue and neglect what ought to be regarded and treated as an instrument for impressing the minds of men, more potent, more tenderly effectual, than all the prepared and prescribed forms that were ever made ready to their hands.

And, as I hope that the consciences of some will be roused by what has been said, to a more just estimate of this whole subject than they have heretofore made; so I trust they will see that no essential improvement will be likely to be made in this department of the public service without serious and devoted attention to the subject; without a governing desire to excel; without much communion with the Father of our spirits, and his Son Jesus Christ; and without unceasing application for help from on high. I hesitate not, once more, to apply to this attainment those emphatic words which our Master in heaven applied to another—'This kind goeth not out, but by prayer and fasting' (Matt. 17:21).

THE END

BANNER *of* TRUTH

The Banner of Truth Trust originated in 1957 in London. The founders believed that much of the best literature of historic Christianity had been allowed to fall into oblivion and that, under God, its recovery could well lead not only to a strengthening of the church, but to true revival.

Inter-denominational in vision, this publishing work is now international, and our lists include a number of contemporary authors along with classics from the past. The translation of these books into many languages is encouraged.

A monthly magazine, *The Banner of Truth*, is also published. More information about this and all our publications can be found on our website or supplied by either of the offices below.

Head Office:
3 Murrayfield Road
Edinburgh
EH12 6EL
United Kingdom
Email: info@banneroftruth.co.uk

North America Office:
PO Box 621
Carlisle, PA 17013
United States of America
Email: info@banneroftruth.org